SALLY FIELD

SALLY FIELD

Jason Bonderoff

ST. MARTIN'S PRESS
New York

Library of Congress Cataloging-in-Publication Data

Bonderoff, Jason.
  Sally Field.

    1. Field, Sally. 2. Moving-picture actors and actresses—United States—Biography. I. Title.
PN2287.F43B66   1987   791.43'028'0924 [B]   87-13107
ISBN 0-312-01086-9

First Edition

10 9 8 7 6 5 4 3 2 1

Contents

A selection of photographs follows page 64.

1. Look Back in Anger

A pint-size Doris Day. Little Miss Gidget-Two-Shoes. The Flying Airhead. The Eternal Beach Bunny. The Last American Virgin . . .

For years that's what Hollywood called Sally Field, and no matter how hard she battled to prove herself as a Serious Actress—and a Serious Woman—the snide nicknames stuck. She once confided to an interviewer that she felt trapped behind her "cutesy, smiley, all-American, girl-next-door face," but how could she escape from the bondage of Kewpie-doll charisma? Short of undergoing some kind of reverse plastic-surgery to chisel away every last vestige of perkiness, there wasn't much that Sally could do about her looks—or her perennial school-girl image.

Even her five-year romance with Burt Reynolds left something to be desired. If the question on "The Hollywood Squares" was "What kind of wild and wicked drink do Burt and Sally remind you of?" the answer was more likely to be "hot chocolate" than a "Harvey Wallbanger." Nevertheless, the public idolized them, and viewed Sally as a steadying influence in Reynolds's often stormy life.

The tabloids were quick to dramatize the Florence Nightingale aspect of the romance, harping on the idea that Sally was Burt's guardian angel and nursemaid, not just another one of his back-lot concubines. Undoubtedly, there was some truth to that. Illness had played an important part in the relationship right from the beginning. When they first met in 1977, on the set of *Smokey and the Bandit*, Burt was suffering from hypoglycemia (low blood sugar), which left him prone to debilitating bouts of depression and fatigue, if he didn't watch his diet. Sally hovered over him like a mother coddling a sick child. She invariably caught him when he tried to sneak-eat forbidden foods and nagged him when he didn't get enough rest. Sister Bertrille on "The Flying Nun" couldn't have fluffed up his pillows with more aplomb!

Even when they broke up in 1982, Sally remained a model of cheerful resignation. The breakup hurt bitterly, but she kept her thoughts—and her anger—to herself. Hiding her feelings—not venting them—has always been her first reaction in times of stress.

Only rarely does Sally's dark side show through. In 1979, on the set of *Back Roads,* she got into a nasty fight with co-star Tommy Lee Jones and sank her teeth into his hand. Shortly before that, while making *Beyond the Poseidon Adventure,* Sally insulted director Irwin Allen in front of the whole crew. Even on *Norma Rae*—a film she loved making—things accidentally got out of hand, and Sally inadvertently wound up injuring two other actors. It happened during a climactic brawl scene, when five-foot, three-inch Sally, who weighs barely more than a hundred pounds, pushed one actor so hard that she knocked him across the room, and he fell and broke his rib. The actor he landed on came out of that scene with a hairline fracture. Afterward, director Martin Ritt, who actually adored Sally, told her, "It's shocking that somebody who looks like you can have such anger." Unintentional though the incident was, it left a strong impression.

The anger has been there all her life, along with the mood swings and the insecurity. But for most of her forty years, Sally has managed to keep all her demons bottled up. In fact, like many successful artists, she long ago became a master of the game. Early on she learned the secret: how to hide her anger in her work. It explains how she could transform herself into TV's Sybil, a multiple-personality schizophrenic with a dozen-plus exquisitely bizarre character twists, or the movie character Norma Rae, one of the angriest women ever to emerge on-screen.

Occasionally, at times when her own life has veered sharply away from sitcom and verged on sadness, a few holes have worn through her gingham image. In 1982, Sally went to Europe—alone—to promote her new movie, *Absence of Malice*. She was thirty-five and divorced, feeling very much at loose ends. Her relationship with Burt Reynolds was over (for better or for worse), and her mother and kids were back home in California. She couldn't bear to stay in her hotel room at night, yet after being sheltered for so many years—first by her husband, later by Burt—she didn't know the first thing about how to go about meeting men. All day long there were interviews, photo sessions, and a round of other promotional appearances to keep her busy—but the evenings were unbearable. She'd come back to her hotel room, restless and still keyed up from the day's activities. She'd call home, order room service, maybe read for a while. Then, suddenly, she couldn't stay in that room any longer. So she'd sit down at her dressing mirror, redo her makeup, twist her hair into a more elaborate coif, then slip into something gorgeous—and expensive—and wander back out into the night. In London, Paris, and Berlin the routine was always the same: Sally would find a noisy bar somewhere and sit there for hours—a lost lady in a faraway city—wrapped in her mink, drinking vodka gimlets and blowing smoke rings seductively in the air. Gidget goes slumming.

"My whole life it's been like this: I've always felt I had to put on a phony face and be sweet and funny," Sally once said. "I was never encouraged to really let my hair down." But inside she always believed that "a savage, green-eyed monster," as she puts it, was waiting to leap out from behind the Pollyanna mask. Her chilling self-appraisal sounds almost like a page from the script of *Sybil,* her acclaimed 1976 TV-movie about a severely disturbed young woman. But while Sybil's mind eventually splintered into sixteen separate personalities, early on Sally found a far more acceptable way to deal with her private pain. As a child, she regularly escaped into fantasy. It was the perfect nourishment for an emotionally hungry future actress.

Sally Margaret Field—the brown-haired, brown-eyed little girl who would grow up to convince the world she was both the angelic Flying Nun and the embittered Norma Rae—was born in Pasadena, California, on November 6, 1946. She grew up in the shadow of the movie studio. Her mother, Maggie, was a former contract player at Paramount; her stepfather, Jock Mahoney, was a Hollywood stuntman turned actor who muscled his way through two *Tarzan* epics, then became the "Range Rider" and "Yancy Derringer" on TV.

Sally was a first-generation Californian. Her father, Richard Field, a San Fernando Valley pharmacist who moved out when Sally was four, was really an Easterner at heart; her mother was a transplanted Southerner. On her mother's side, the entire family had migrated to Los Angeles from Texas, but hadn't shed any of their Southern sensibilities along the way. In many ways her mother, grandmother, and aunts were all resourceful women—survivors. They were reminiscent of Edna Spaulding, the valiant young widow who struggles to save her farm and family in *Places in the Heart*. But among Sally's Texas kin, public displays of bravado weren't considered ladylike. So the women all hid behind a veil of frail gentility. Sally grew up getting mixed signals: On the one hand, be tough; on the other, don't let anyone know how tough you really are. "My grandmother is as strong as they get," Sally once confided to a reporter for *People,* "but you wouldn't know it at first if you sat and talked to her."

Sally and her older brother, Richard, were raised in a house where Southern cooking and Southern accents predominated. But Sally wasn't nearly so interested in learning how to bake cornbread and fry chicken as she was in watching old movies on TV. That was her private world, her sanctuary. As a child, she was enthralled by the antics of Jean Arthur and Carole Lombard, spellbound by the sophisticated savvy of Katharine Hepburn. She loved to spend long afternoons in a darkened room, curled up in front of the TV set, watching the vintage-film "Early Shows" that dominated the local channels.

Sally's reclusiveness was her only defense against the tense atmosphere at home. Her parents' divorce had left her shaken—she never really got over it—and the upheaval of her father's leaving was doubly compounded by a swift change in living arrangements. After the divorce, Sally and her brother Rick were shipped off to live with their grandmother for two years, so Maggie could work full-time.

When Sally was six, her mother married Jock Mahoney, and the family was reunited under one roof. But gaining a stepfather didn't solve all of Sally's problems. There were adjustments to be made, and Jock's arrival only reinforced Sally's vague sense of isolation. Perfect, happy endings, she suspected, were the province of MGM movies, not real life.

Jock—a hulking, six-foot-four super-athlete—was keen on the outdoor life. He taught his stepchildren to swim and horseback ride and hang tough. He was the total opposite of Sally's own father, a quiet, gentle, somewhat sad man whom she dearly missed. Yet, for better or for worse, it was Jock, not her own father, who was primarily responsible for guiding Sally into the world. To be sure, he taught her to be strong and independent, but he also tried to inculcate his rigid, old-fashioned views on relations between the sexes. As she blossomed into a teenager, Jock warned her repeatedly that boys would only want one thing from her—sex—and then they'd never want to see her again. Years later, Sally confided to *Playgirl* correspondent Celeste Fremon that, because of Jock's influence, "the first time I made love, I felt bad, you know. I felt dirty."

Strangely enough, Sally later chose her stepfather's profession—acting—as her own, and despite their differences, she became his child in other ways, too. For all her china-doll veneer, there's a toughness and a stubbornness to Sally Margaret Field—a real scrappy quality—that's often been her lifeline in show business. Even her involvement with Burt Reynolds may have been an unconscious tribute to Jock's influence. In Burt she found a guy who was a real "man's man"—gregarious, rowdy, athletic, and, from a distance at least, slightly larger than life. Like Jock Mahoney, Burt reveled in doing his own movie stunts.

Yet in other ways—in terms of her sensitivity, for example—Sally remained her father's child. And, ironically, even though Richard Field was the only one of her parents who was *not* an actor, he helped push her toward a show-business career, too. His absence left a void in her life that only fantasy and make-believe could fill.

Sally's passion for old movies actually started the same time that her father left. Interestingly enough, one of her favorite films—both then and now—was *The Awful Truth,* a 1937 comedy-drama about a divorcing couple (Irene Dunne and Cary Grant) who make plans to marry other people, but eventually realize they're still in love and reconcile. It was the perfect happy ending for her own parents, one that reality couldn't provide. But other films and other stars captured her imagination, too. Lying on the floor in front of the TV, hugging a maroon comforter and hanging on every breezy word of dialogue, Sally began to imagine herself stepping into Kate Hepburn's shoes in *Woman of the Year* or carrying off Carole Lombard's harebrained antics in *My Man Godfrey.*

Then she'd go to her room to act out her fantasies. By her own admission, she was shy and didn't have many friends; Sally much preferred the company of her make-believe movie casts to dolls or other children. "I liked staying in my room alone, with the door shut, pretending to be whatever I wanted," she remembers. "It was the only place I felt free to cry or sing or get angry and kick things around. In front of other people, I was always expected to be a well-behaved little girl—no fussiness or sour faces, please. My private movie world was the only place where I could get out all those bad feelings I had stored up inside me."

Years later, in characterizations like Norma Rae (the fire-breathing union organizer), Megan Carter (the hard-boiled reporter in *Absence of Malice*), and Amy Post (the itinerant hooker in *Back Roads*), Sally finally found a positive outlet for all her "bad feelings." In 1984, she publicly acknowledged what seemed like a rather strange attitude: that anger had always been her best friend. "The anger comes from an accumulation of years of letting myself be treated disrespectfully," she told *The Los Angeles Times*. It came partially from her early home, where she'd been forced to toe such a tough line, and partially from work. Making "The Flying Nun" when she was barely twenty-one took its toll on her. Despite the show's long-running TV success, it was a demoralizing experience for Sally, and the scars are still there. In Hollywood, even on the set itself, she was made to feel like a bad joke, and Sally was too young and too intimidated to fight back. The Hollywood smart set shunned—or ridiculed—her because her TV image wasn't hip enough, or political enough, for the new down-with-the-Establishment dogma of the late 1960s. If only Sister Bertrille rode a motorcycle, bad-mouthed the police and got arrested once in a while!

For her own part, Sally felt incredibly frustrated by roles like Gidget and The Flying Nun, but she didn't know how to make the quantum leap from teen star to dramatic actress. "I was burning to play Juliet and Cleopatra," she once said. "But after 'The Flying Nun,' Hollywood decided that 'cute' was all I could ever be. The only scripts they offered me were comedies where I'd play somebody's cute wife or cute girlfriend."

Sally's introduction to the arts had come directly from her mother, who'd read Shakespeare and Chekhov aloud to her as a baby. "She gave me my theater instincts," Sally acknowledges. "My earliest memories are of being bundled up in a blanket and taken to Charles Laughton's acting class." Maggie Mahoney, in fact, was one of Laughton's most promising students, but she made little effort to pursue a theatrical career. "She was talented, but at a certain point she just stopped working," Sally once told reporter Paul Rosenfield. "A place in her just shut down." After Maggie's marriage to Jock, her family life took priority. Occasionally, she worked in grade-B movies like *The Man From Planet X,* but mainly she contented herself with raising her children—Sally, Rick, and their half-sister, Princess, who was born in 1953.

Tending her brood—while her husband's career occupied the limelight—felt perfectly natural to Maggie Mahoney. She was a woman of her time and place. Moreover, keeping her feelings in check was a strong part of her Southern heritage. Sally later complained that her mother never got angry or depressed in front of her. In print, she referred to that "Mother Knows Best" image as a "loving, supportive . . . robot." Sally also laughed that her mother's notion of ideal womanhood was a gazelle in petticoats who "glided around the lawn and never peed behind the garage."

But for all her shortcomings, Sally's mother was also her quiet tower of strength, her biggest booster, and—*possibly*—her best friend. "My mom gave me self-worth, that attitude that if I failed or did something awful, or if people laughed, it didn't matter." In 1980, when Sally stepped onstage to receive her first Academy Award, for *Norma Rae,* she acknowledged her mother's friendship as the cornerstone of her success.

As a youngster, Sally was also close to her older brother, Rick. They were both dreamers, but their vehicles of expression were very different. While Sally preferred playacting in front of a mirror, Rick was usually busy tinkering with a chemistry or Erector set. Later, at Berkeley, he was a straight-A student, a varsity gymnast, and eventually went on to become a highly respected research physicist at the

California Institute of Technology. During his high-school days, Rick was Sally's closest friend. "I'd go to him with all my problems," she recalls. "After I'd come home from a date, I'd sit up half the night talking with him."

To a certain extent, Rick was a substitute for their absentee father, who had long since remarried and built a new life for himself. Richard Field Sr. lived nearby in Temple City (a Los Angeles suburb) with his second wife, Peggy, and their daughter, Shirley, but he kept in touch with Rick and Sally. He occasionally took them on outings. Sally remembers trips to the Santa Anita racetrack—and infrequent picnics—but, by her own admission, she and her father were not exceptionally close. As a teenager, she rarely went to him with her problems—unless they involved her mother and stepfather. But she did look forward to his Christmas and birthday gifts. Her father and stepmother invariably bought her something pink and feminine, while her stepfather Jock's idea of a gift was, as Sally put it, "something kooky."

Sally was nine years older than her stepsister, Shirley, but made every effort to get along with her. Shirley was only eleven when Sally's first TV series, "Gidget," aired, and was very impressed by it all. At the time, Sally told the press: "She's a cute kid and my best critic. Shirley watches 'Gidget' every week and then tells me what she and her girlfriends like about it."

On the home front, Sally's stepfather—"Jocko," as she called him—ruled the roost. He was the epitome of the macho ethic, and firmly entrenched in his very traditional beliefs about women. He was also far more the disciplinarian than Sally's mother, and worked hard at cultivating qualities of physical and emotional toughness in his kids. "He's preparing me for the world," Sally once said. He was the first to encourage her to stand up to her teachers, and later to her agents and directors. When Sally started dating, he hovered at the front door like The Incredible Hulk. "Every boy who came to the house was scared to death at first," Sally said. "They were put off by this big, muscular man and the loudness of his voice. Jocko would be very cordial, but the poor boys would just stand there with their knees rattling. They'd stutter every time they answered a question."

The fact that Jocko was a former stuntman—and a real daredevil—left an indelible impression on his stepdaughter. Sally grew up believing that she always had to be unafraid, that she constantly had to prove herself to Jocko. Years later, in fact, when Sally and Burt Reynolds collaborated on *Hooper,* a movie that celebrated the uproarious side of Hollywood stuntwork, the character of the aging stunt king—played by Brian Keith—was based on Jock Mahoney.

While Jock had rather fixed ideas about sex, marriage, and women, he was very open-minded where religion was concerned. He never encouraged any of the children to go to a specific church. When Princess was seven, she suddenly announced that she wanted to become Jewish. At the time, the Mahoneys were living in a predominantly Jewish neighborhood, and Jock realized that Princess's sudden impulse probably came from just wanting to be accepted. So for a month Jock took her to Saturday services at a synagogue—long enough for all her friends to see her there. Later, when the Mahoneys moved on to a Catholic neighborhood, Princess suddenly developed a great interest in Catholicism. So Jock started taking her to Mass—again, just long enough for her to start to feel comfortable in the neighborhood. A while later, Princess learned that she was part Cherokee; this sparked a new surge of religious fervor. She quickly abandoned both Judaism and Catholicism in favor of her Indian heritage. "Luckily," Jock recalled, "there was no Cherokee church nearby, so I didn't have to start taking her to those services, too."

Jock tried to be a good father—he exerted a strong influence over Princess as well as Maggie's two children—but somehow, where Sally was concerned, a wall always remained. In an interview with writer Aimee Lee Ball, Sally once confided that Jock's treatment of her was partially responsible for her loneliness as an adult, her inability to let people get too close. Closeness, after all, means risk. There's always the possibility of getting hurt. And that's what Sally was determned to shield herself from. She felt that Jock had disappointed her. She remembered how many times he'd let her down as a child—little things, like promising to take her to a drive-in movie on Saturday and then forgetting. "To me, that was a trip to Switzerland," she said. "And then he would think so little of it that he'd change his mind. And I was demolished."

As a child, Sally was molded by the two most important men in her life—her father and stepfather—yet strangely cut off from them both. It was a theme that would recede for a time, then reappear to haunt her over and over again through the years: Her stepfather, whom she wanted to idolize, turned out to be flawed and human; her father, whom she needed to love, was no longer there. And so, without realizing it, she was searching for an anchor. When she was fourteen, she found him. In eight years she would marry him.

2. Francine "Gidget" Lawrence

In the late 1950s, Portola Junior High School was the kind of place where Francine "Gidget" Lawrence would have felt right at home—but Sally Field, who later immortalized Gidget, remained somewhat of an outsider all through her stay there. She earned good grades and threw herself into all kinds of social activities—she even went out for cheerleading—but popularity continued to elude her. The only thing that saved her from total adolescent despair was dramatics—that's where Sally found a place to shine. She managed to wangle a part in nearly every school production.

Years later she confided to an interviewer from *The Chicago Tribune,* "I almost didn't make it out of school because of dramatics. I just ran the whole department. I was like a monster someone had created." Her grades suffered a bit from all the time and energy she was pouring into her new-found theatrical life, but her mother, who was Sally's staunchest ally at home, refused to discourage her. Jock, on the other hand, took a little more convincing.

In eighth grade, Sally was chosen to do three scenes from *Romeo and Juliet* on Parents' Night. Jock said little, but her mother was visibly impressed. Afterwards, she told Sally, "I'm beginning to think you have magic." That's all Sally needed to hear: She was off and running!

Nevertheless, "stardom" didn't open many doors for her socially. Through her performances, she gained a few fans at school, but no close friends. At the age of thirteen she felt "weird" and "different than the other kids." In school her favorite retreat was the girls' bathroom. She'd hide out in a stall—away from all the other kids—and whisper over and over again to herself, "You're a good person . . . You're a good person."

But in a way Sally wasn't so different from everyone else, even if her dreams of stardom weren't quite the norm. She was still a teenager; and like teenagers everywhere, she was trying hard to assert her own identity—yet she was desperate to "fit in." "When I was fourteen, right after junior-high-school graduation, I went to the beach every day," she recalls. "It was the thing to do that summer. If you didn't go to the beach, you were out of it."

The purpose of that time-honored California ritual was to be surrounded by as many older boys as possible. "You didn't pick them up, you just looked," is how Sally remembers it. But Sally, who was small for her age, had a hard time of it. Some of the other girls shunned her, complaining that Sally was so young-looking she'd cramp their style and drive the boys away. On top of that, Sally was recovering from minor foot surgery that summer, so she couldn't even go in the water. But her semi-invalid condition turned out to be a blessing in disguise. On one occasion, a group of high-school boys took pity on her and spent the whole afternoon teaching her to play cards.

During her first year at Birmingham High School, Sally began to blossom. She came out of her cocoon and landed a boyfriend—Steve Craig. He was sixteen, an upperclassman, and considered a prize catch. At first glance, Sally decided that Steve and his friends were the most gorgeous-looking group of boys in the whole school—but totally unattainable. They were wickedly funny, very popular, and very sure of themselves. A friend warned Sally to steer clear of them—"Watch out, those boys just want to tease you!" she said. Luckily, Sally didn't listen. At a football game Steve kept trying to convince her to go out with a buddy of his; she kept turning the arrangement down. Finally, Steve said in exasperation, "You know, you aren't so bad; maybe I'll take you out myself."

And that's how Sally and her future husband, Steve Craig, became sweethearts at Birmingham High. But the romance didn't exactly get off to a flying start. For all his outward self-confidence, Steve was a little uneasy about going steady. For the first month they dated, he kept totally ignoring Sally at school. He'd give her the cold shoulder every time he bumped into her in the hall. Sally liked him a lot, but his behavior was infuriating. Finally, she got up the nerve to confront him. She called him on the phone—shaking all over because she'd never called a boy before—and told him that she never wanted to see him again. Instead of getting angry, he started laughing. No girl had ever stood up to him like that before. And Sally's feistiness paid off. After that, Steve made it a point to be much more considerate of Sally's feelings.

After graduation, Sally was slated to enroll at Valley State College, right in L.A., but first she convinced Jock and Maggie to let her take a summer workshop at Columbia Studios. "It was just a little acting class that met one night a week—something to keep me busy till college began," Sally recalls.

But it turned out to be a far more crucial step than either Sally or her parents had bargained for.

One night Eddie Foy III, a casting director for Screen Gems, came to observe the class. When the workshop ended and Sally was outside waiting for her brother Rick to pick her up, Foy came over and struck up a conversation.

"Aren't you Jock Mahoney's daughter?" he asked.

"Yes," replied Sally, who was too dumbstruck to say much else.

He asked her about her acting ambitions, and Sally mumbled a few words in response.

She was so nervous, she recalls, that she was shaking like a leaf. "He probably thught I was a drug addict or something," she laughs. "I was so terrified that all my words kept jumbling together."

Nevertheless, Sally must have made a reasonably good impression on the man. He asked her to come to his office the next day for an interview.

Sally barely slept a wink that night, and the next day she showed up, right on time, accompanied by her stepfather. She happened to be wearing cutoffs, a T-shirt, and sandals because she planned on heading out to the beach right after the interview, but she couldn't have chosen a more perfect outfit if she'd tried. When Sally walked through the door, Foy's first reaction was: "She's the perfect Gidget"—and that's exactly the part he sent her out to audition for.

Ironically, although Sally would become most identified with the role in the public's mind, she wasn't the first actress to portray America's favorite teenager. In 1959 Sandra Dee had starred in the original movie, with Cliff Robertson and James Darren as two beach-blanket Romeos competing for her affections. In 1961 Deborah Walley replaced her in the sequel, *Gidget Goes Hawaiian,* and two years later a third

Gidget—Cindy Carol—appeared on the scene, in yet another big-screen follow-up, *Gidget Goes to Rome*.

Those surfside seduction epics were the backbone of the drive-in movie circuit, and Sally herself had been raised on them. She was nearly thirteen when the first movie came out, and she saw it nine times. "My friends and I would all go sit in a row," Sally recalls, "and say, 'Oh, isn't Sandra Dee lucky! Just look at James Darren, he's so cute!' It was absolutely *the* movie to see." By the time *Gidget Goes Hawaiian* premiered, Sally's tastes were beginning to mature a bit, and she saw that film only three times. And when *Gidget Goes to Rome* came along, Sally was almost seventeen and much more interested in movies like *Tom Jones* and *Hud* than teen-age-*angst* stories. Suddenly, James Darren couldn't hold a candle to Albert Finney and Paul Newman. In fact, she didn't even care if Gidget got pinched on the Spanish Steps or not!

Nevertheless, despite her own disenchantment with the world according to Sandra Dee, Sally was destined to transform herself into Francine "Gidget" Lawrence—a teenager whose main mission in life was to find "endless fun in the sun"—in the ABC television series. The show, which debuted on September 15, 1965 (opposite ABC's "Beverly Hillbillies"), ran for one season on the air. Don Porter co-starred as Gidget's widowed father, Professor Russ Lawrence, and Lynette Winter played her best friend and fellow sun-and-fun seeker, Larue.

Sally won the role after beating out seventy-five other actresses in a grueling series of auditions. She had no qualms about accepting the role. Doing "Gidget" meant putting her college plans on hold, but starring in her own weekly television series was definitely too golden an opportunity to pass up. When production started, Sally was a total novice on the set, but her TV father, Don Porter, took her under his wing. He taught her all about camera angles and how to find her mark; he even interceded on her behalf when she had a problem with her dialogue or wardrobe.

"Everyone was very protective of Sally," one of the show's "grips" remembers. "After all, she was just a kid. She was trying hard, but this was all very new to her. She'd never done television before. If she forgot her lines, she was so apologetic—and Screen Gems was incredibly patient with her. She was just what they wanted—a fresh-faced kid they hoped would put some real spunk into the part. They'd hired her for her naturalness, not her technique. The last thing in the world they wanted was a professional child star."

Ironically, although "Gidget" failed as a first-run TV series, it went on to become one of the most popular rerun properties in syndication. Today, more than twenty years later, it still airs in various parts of the country and Sally Field—along with "Father Knows Best"'s Elinor Donahue and "The Donna Reed Show"'s Shelley Fabares—remains as innocent and squeaky-clean as ever, up to her ponytail in perpetual adolescence.

In the 1970s, TV tried to resurrect the "Gidget" theme on several occasions—in the form of made-for-TV-movies—but none of these uninspired sequels seemed to live up to the high standards that Sandra Dee and Sally Field had set for them. In the tele-movie *Gidget Grows Up,* Karen Valentine took over the part. Gidget traded in her bikinis for business suits, moved to New York, and became a tour guide at the United Nations. Two years later, *Gidget Gets Married* found our heroine miraculously transplanted to a split-level suburban development in Glossop, Maryland, where she was a discontented newlywed, married to an upwardly mobile young executive. This time Monie Ellis played the title role. Gidget's last incarnation to date was in 1985, when Caryn Richman starred in *Gidget's Summer Reunion*. Television critic Leonard Maltin summed up the plot in a tidy nutshell: "Another decade, another Gidget, and this time the little surfer's a married travel agent, still looking for the perfect wave. . . ." *Summer Reunion* became the pilot for "The New Gidget," a syndicated TV series.

At this rate, revised and recycled versions of "Gidget" may inundate the airwaves forever. In 1990 the next Gidget may run for President (campaigning on a surfboard, of course) or open a suntan-oil concession on Mars. So much has changed in America since the original movie hit the drive-in circuit in 1959 (whatever happened to drive-ins, anyway?), but obviously there's something universal—and eternally endearing—about this lovable flake. Her charm doesn't wear off.

Ironically, thanks to the magic of television reruns, Sally Field has become more identified with Gidget than any other actress who played the role. Sally was only nineteen when she did the series, and she never expected it would become such an enduring part of her professional biography. At the time, she viewed her television apprenticeship as simply a means to an end—a stepping-stone to what she really wanted—motion-picture stardom. She never dreamed that she'd do two more situation comedies, "The Flying Nun" and "The Girl With Something Extra," in quick succession after "Gidget." No, she was ready for bigger things; she fully intended to carry on where Jean Arthur and Carole Lombard had left off. The silver screen was going to be her metier, she was sure of that.

As it turned out, though, Sally didn't move into the motion-picture arena till she was thirty years old. For the time being, she was doomed to remain in the weekly TV series grind—a circumstance that, despite her enormous success, was basically anathema to her. Yet, later, she had to admit that her TV sojourn hadn't entirely been a waste of time; the four seasons grinding out weekly episodes of "Gidget" and "The Flying Nun" had proven to be a valuable training ground. "Those series didn't hurt me," she conceded to journalist Bob Lardine. "They gave me the greatest education in the world. There isn't anything I can't do in front of a TV camera as a result of the experience I gained from them. I could stand on my head right now if necessary and spit wooden nickels."

"Gidget" not only became Sally's ticket to professional employment in Hollywood, it set the wheels in motion for the future. Even though the show was canceled, her own fledgling career gained momentum. Right after the series ended, Sally co-starred in *Take Her, She's Mine,* with Walter Pidgeon, at the Valley Music Theater in Los Angeles; then came guest-starring roles on two TV series—"Occasional Wife" and "Hey, Landlord"—and a featured role in the 1967 movie *The Way West,* with Kirk Douglas, Robert Mitchum, and Richard Widmark.

1967—the year she turned twenty-one—was a turning point in Sally's life. She left Jock and Maggie's house and moved into her own apartment in Malibu (Sally was so nervous that her mother had to spend the first night with her), and she began to think about the possibility of a real movie career. Her hopes escalated when she screen-tested for the part of Dustin Hoffman's girlfriend in the new Mike Nichols film, *The Graduate,* but her euphoria was short-lived. Nichols decided to hire Katharine Ross instead. The reason was simple: Sally had no movie experience (except for her small role in *The Way West*) and, despite the cancellation of her show, she was still very much identified with "Gidget."

Katharine, on the other hand, was a little more mature and a lot more camera-wise. Three years older than Sally, Katharine had already appeared in four films: *The Singing Nun, Shenandoah, Mr. Buddwing,* and *Games.*

All this time Sally had still been dating Steve Craig on a semi-exclusive basis. In high school, they'd gone steady (much to Jock and Maggie's chagrin), but once Steve was enrolled at USC and Sally's TV career began to take off, their two different worlds began to pull them apart. Most of Sally's other "romances" were studio-arranged publicity events, but they accomplished exactly what Screen Gems wanted—they made headlines. Sally was regularly photographed on the town with Peter Deuel, Chris George, Paul Peterson, and Jerry Lewis's son Gary. Despite their mutual agreement that they could see other people, it made Steve Craig more than a little jealous. "Steve doesn't like it at all, especially if they're actors," Sally confided, "yet I'm pretty understanding when he goes out with other girls. Maybe I don't mind it so much because I don't know who they are— they're not people in the public eye."

Most of her VIP escorts were "older men"—some of them were even pushing thirty. Peter Deuel, who was twenty-seven, marveled at Sally's maturity. "She's the first young woman I've known who acts her age," he announced. "Most twenty-one-year-olds try to act like they're thirty-five, which makes them dismal flops as far as I'm concerned. Sally's a very refreshing change."

Sally was definitely enchanted by Peter, too, but pretty soon she found another suitor on her doorstep—Gary Lewis. "Gary's so funny," Sally confided. "Whenever we go out, he has me in stitches. But I made the mistake of trying to compete with him by tellling jokes, too. I don't think that appealed to him very much. He's a lot like his dad—he has to be onstage all the time. I guess I shouldn't have tried to top him. Maybe that's why he hasn't called back."

Sally herself was still a novice at the publicity game—and not very comfortable around the superstar set. "If I'm at a party and Paul Newman or Sean Connery walks into the room, I just melt right into the background," Sally confided. "Later on, I always see pictures of myself in the movie magazines—I'm the one all the way over on the side, just standing around and gawking."

One day she was introduced to Omar Sharif on the studio lot. "I was so excited, I almost passed out!" she later admitted to one of the fan magazines that constantly pestered her for interviews. Sharif invited her to visit him on the set of *Funny Girl,* which was filming right down the block, but Sally declined the invitation. "I was too chicken to go," she later revealed. "I was afraid a guard might stop me at the door and say, 'Hey, what do you want, kid?' I may have had my own TV show, but I don't really think of myself as somebody special."

Maybe that's what drew her back to Steve Craig. Even though she was meeting sophisticated leading men—the cream of the movie crop—Sally felt more comfortable with a boy closer to her own age. "I'd never want to marry a much older man," she joked. "It's too risky. He might be dead by the time I'm thirty!" Nor was she interested in playing Liz Taylor to anyone's Richard Burton. "I'd never want to marry an actor," she swore. "They're much too insecure. I'd rather settle down with a good, steady plumber or doctor." (On that count, too, Steve certainly filled the bill: He was a pre-med major at USC.)

During the latter half of 1967, emotional and professional security became particularly important to Sally. After losing out on *The Graduate* (it hurt even more when Katharine

Ross garnered an Oscar nomination for her portrayal of Elaine Robinson), Sally reluctantly agreed to do "The Flying Nun," her second television series. She also put the idea of college permanently on hold.

At a time when college students everywhere were protesting the Vietnam war and social injustice—and rocking to the beat of the Beatles and the new "electric" Bob Dylan—Sally, through the isolating nature of her work, was cut off from the youth culture of the time. She was isolated from almost everything that was happening in the sixties. Never having experienced it, she simply never caught on to what was happening to her age-peers, and thus, never absorbed it. To this day, her taste in music and literature is distinctly middle-of-the-road and surprisingly mild for someone who can summon up so much anger and vehemence in her acting life. Her tastes, "straight" though they may be, reveal a soul with a heightened sense of romance, fantasy, loss, and irony: Her favorite singers are Johnny Mathis and Ella Fitzgerald; her favorite book is a collection of Dorothy Parker stories.

For a long time, Sally was intimidated by her own superficial TV image, by the fact that she'd never gone to college. She allowed herself to be defined by the inanities and clichés of her weekly TV scripts. When Celeste Fremon, an interviewer for *Playgirl*, approached her about a "think piece" in 1983, Sally was in turmoil. "I feel about as fascinating as an ingrown toenail," she said. "I don't have *any* information. I hardly know where Lebanon *is*, you know?"

3. Sister Bertrille:
"A Nun With Sex Appeal"

In 1966 Max Wylie, a man who specialized in developing new television series, had lunch with LeBaron R. Barker, a top editor at Doubleday. The conversation veered toward books that might have TV potential, and Barker mentioned *The Fifteenth Pelican,* a little-known novel Doubleday had published the year before. It was the story of a nun who weighed ninety pounds and flew. Barker thought it would make a terrific television series.

The author of the book, Tere Rios, was a half-Irish, half-Puerto Rican housewife, living in Madison, Wisconsin, who had three published novels to her credit. She was also a former pilot in the Georgia Civil Air Patrol, which explained her interest in aerodynamics. The idea of a "flying nun" had first sprung into her mind many years before she actually wrote the book, when she was in Paris and saw a Sister of Charity in a wide-brimmed white bonnet nearly blown off her feet by a strong gust of wind. The picture of the jet-propelled nun stayed with her and eventually became the basis for Sister Bertrille, the disarming young heroine of *The Fifteenth Pelican.* And if Sister Bertrille seemed slightly more rambunctious than the stereotypical nun, that was precisely Tere Rios's intention. She'd known nuns all her life, and few of them, she claimed, were the absolutely mirthless characters so often depicted in movies and literature. In writing the book, she wanted to set the record straight.

When *The Fifteenth Pelican* hit the bookstores, nuns were definitely enjoying a new vogue in the entertainment world. *The Sound of Music* was breaking records at the box office and Soeur Sourire—the world-famous Singing Nun—had become a chart-buster with her folksy, guitar-strumming rendition of *Dominique*. Not since Ingrid Bergman lifted her eyes to heaven in *The Bells of St. Mary's* had Americans of all religious denominations been so fascinated by Roman Catholic monastic life.

After reading *The Fifteenth Pelican,* Max Wylie was sure he could capitalize on this sudden public interest. Nevertheless, there were obstacles. The networks had no problem with Sister Bertrille's aerodynamically designed headgear—after all, this was 1966, when comedy and fantasy were practically synonomous. Barbara Eden had just popped out of a bottle on "I Dream of Jeannie" and Elizabeth Montgomery was a lovable sorceress on "Bewitched," and those shows were two of TV's biggest hits. No, the problem with "The Flying Nun" (as *The Fifteenth Pelican* was soon renamed for television consumption) was the religious aspect of the show. Sister Bertrille's flights of fancy verged on the miraculous—and miracles were no laughing matter as far as the Catholic Church was concerned. Moreover, would the public at large sit still for a comedy show with spiritual overtones, or would they find it too preachy and discomforting?

Nearly every TV studio in Hollywood rejected the project. William Dozier, producer of "Batman," wasn't interested; programming heads at CBS, Warner Brothers, and MGM all thought the religious problems in the script outweighed the comedy. Leonard Goldberg, who was vice-president in charge of programming at ABC, was adamant: He didn't want the show on his fall schedule. The project might easily have fallen by the wayside if Harry Ackerman, producer of "Bewitched," hadn't taken a liking to it. Ackerman and Screen Gems were looking for a new property for Sally Field after "Gidget" went off the air; Ackerman believed that "The Flying Nun" would be the perfect vehicle for her, and he eventually convinced ABC's Goldberg to change his mind.

Bernard Slade, a Canadian comedy writer who'd done a lot of scripting on "Bewitched," was given the job of developing "The Flying Nun" into a viable TV property. Slade, a Protestant, wasn't thrilled by the prospect. He didn't think the initial idea was funny at all. Ironically, his wife, who was Catholic, thought the idea was "cute."

Yet once Harry Ackerman and Screen Gems, the company he was associated with, had a tentative commitment from ABC to accept the project, Screen Gems began making a concerted effort to get the approval of the Catholic Church. Rosalind Wyman, a former Los Angeles councilwoman, was hired as a lobbyist on their behalf. The thrust of her publicity campaign was that, far from denigrating nuns and their way of life, "The Flying Nun" would actually perform a tremendous service: It would show America how the Church was changing and modernizing itself. Private screenings of the pilot were arranged for three key figures—Cardinal McIntyre of Los Angeles, Cardinal Spellman of New York, and Archbishop Hannan of New Orleans. As it turned out, Ackerman and company had worried for nothing. The prelates were all delighted with the show. Because it was so warm and appealing, they saw it as a great recruitment poster; they were particularly pleased that it humanized nuns.

With that obstacle out of the way, there was only one problem left: The show was about to go on the air minus a leading lady. Up until the last minute, Sally Field refused to play the role.

From the beginning, Ackerman and Screen Gems executives envisioned only one actress as Sister Bertrille—and that actress was Sally Field. They had absolute faith in her ability to play "a nun with sex appeal" without sinking into slapstick or camp. In fact, they nicknamed her "Sister Terrific," because that's exactly the kind of screen persona they expected Sally to create when shooting began.

But "Sister Terrific" wasn't interested in creating any persona at all. At first she turned down the role because she hated the idea—she was certain it would be a disaster. After her failure in "Gidget," Sally had no wish to involve herself in another TV flop. "Besides, I didn't want to play a nun," Sally told *TV Guide*. "You're not allowed to kiss or show your bellybutton."

Instead, she was determined to hold out for more-serious roles—and she had no great love for her former bosses at Screen Gems. She was still angry over the way she'd been treated when "Gidget" was canceled. Nobody had even bothered to call and tell her the show had been axed. The studio's lack of courtesy had left Sally feeling that maybe they blamed her for the show's failure, and for a while her confidence was completely shot. It took her a long time to get over "Gidget." She'd been so distraught, in fact, that she'd stayed home for a month, not pursuing her career at all. Then, tired of hibernating and feeling sorry for herself, she'd pulled herself together and gone back out on casting interviews. Now, just when she'd put "Gidget" behind her, Screen Gems was coming back to haunt her.

OUTREACH Threshold, Day Service – Lonnie
53076
Unclaim : 1/25/2021

Held date   : 1/18/2021
Pickup location : West Bend Outreach Branch

Title   : Sally Field
Call number   : BIO FIE-S B64
Item barcode   : 33357000814728
Assigned branch : West Bend Community Memorial Library

Notes: Outreach Services Patron

Bookmobile Stop: WEST BEND SENIOR DAY SERVICE

Sally was testing for *The Graduate* at approximately the same time Screen Gems was pursuing her to do "The Flying Nun," which may also account for her standoffishness. But even if the movie hadn't been clouding the picture, Sally still would have been stubbornly resistant to this project. She didn't particularly care for Ackerman's way of treating her. He refused to deal with her directly, transmitting all his contract offers through her stepfather and her agent, Herb Tobias. Sally didn't like being kept in the dark; it made her feel like a child. The situation, as far as she was concerned, was turning into "Gidget" all over again. Perhaps, if Ackerman had made a greater effort to deal with her on a one-to-one basis, Sally might have knuckled under and accepted the job much sooner.

At any rate, when shooting began on the "Flying Nun" pilot in December 1966, Sally remained mysteriously unavailable. "Emergency" star Bobby Troup's daughter, Ronne, was hurriedly brought in to play Sister Bertrille. If Sally had continued to boycott the set, she probaby would have gone on to do the series, too. (Actually, Ronne Troup had a rather short-lived TV career. Her only major credit after this was a two-year stint on "My Three Sons" as Chip's girlfriend, Polly.)

While production of the pilot was in progress, line producer Bill Sackheim decided to make one last attempt to get through to Sally. Realizing that hurt feelings—not money or movie offers—might be the real root of the problem, he invited her to come down to his office for a chat. His approach—a little old-fashioned ego-stroking—apparently did the trick.

The very fact that Sackheim made the gesture, by calling her directly, meant the world to Sally. It was the one element that had been missing in her negotiations with his boss, Ackerman. As Sally later explained to *TV Guide,* Sack-

heim "understood that losing 'Gidget' was like having someone call your kids ugly," and he knew how to make her feel
wanted again. He also made her realize that it was too soon
to think about crossing over to films. That juncture was still
a few years down the line, when she had more acting experience under her belt. And that's what "The Flying Nun"
would give her—the one thing she needed most—experience. "I told myself, you're not Liz Taylor!" she explained to
TV Guide's Dwight Whitney. "'The Flying Nun' would give
me time to learn and still keep me in the public eye."

In the end, Sally's holdout had one hidden fringe benefit—it upped the ante on her contract considerably. Sally
had earned only $450 a week when she was doing "Gidget,"
but Screen Gems was willing to go a little higher when they
offered her "The Flying Nun." They first tempted her with a
salary of $1,500 a week, then raised that figure to $2,000.
By the time she finally signed on as Sister Bertrille, Screen
Gems had to shell out $4,000 a week in order to get her.

According to Jackie Cooper, who was Screen Gems' production chief at that time, Sally probably would have been
willing to work for $1,500 an episode—and would have
agreed to do the show much sooner—if the studio brass
hadn't kept dragging their feet. In his autobiography, *Please
Don't Shoot My Dog,* Jackie appraises the whole confusing
affair from an entirely different angle: He takes credit for
optioning *The Fifteenth Pelican* in the first place (he did it for
under $40,000) and for immediately targeting it as a future
project for Sally Field. "She was doing 'Gidget' for us," he
writes, "but I knew that wasn't going to make it. I also had a
feeling that Sally was going to be a big star and felt we
should keep her under contract, and to do that, we had to
have a property . . . that's why I optioned 'The Flying
Nun.'"

But the front office in New York saw red. Jerry Hyams, president of Screen Gems, and John Mitchell, the sales manager, were both opposed to the idea of an aerodynamically inspired TV nun—and to the idea of Sally Field playing her—and they forced Jackie Cooper to break off contract negotiations with Sally. He enlisted the aid of Tom Moore, an ABC executive, to plead his case, and eventually, thanks to Moore's intervention, Hyams and Mitchell changed their minds. By that time, however, Sally—and her agent—were no longer interested in $1,500 an episode. Their price had now risen dramatically.

Screen Gems incurred even more extra costs by having to reshoot part of the pilot (in which Ronne Troupe appeared), but despite all the delays and complications, "The Flying Nun" made it onto ABC's fall schedule, and enjoyed a respectable three-season run, moving from Thursday night to Wednesday night to Friday night. Although the show never became a top-20 Nielsen hit, it developed a strong following, especially among teenagers, who idolized Sally Field.

The show took place in the Convent San Tanco in a picturesque corner of old San Juan. Sister Bertrille was a young novice who possessed the uncanny ability to fly whenever a strong wind got hold of the broad brim of her white coronet. There was nothing really miraculous about Sister Bertrille's unique, self-propelled mode of transportation—it had more to do with her own light weight and certain obscure laws of physics than any beneficent act of Heaven. As Sister Bertrille often explained it, "When lift plus thrust is greater than load plus drag, watch out!"

Sister Bertrille's airborne adventures were more in the tradition of Lucy Ricardo than Amelia Earhardt. Sometimes she wound up tangled in a tree or floating in the Caribbean. Once a pelican mistook her for an exotic bird and fell in love with her; in another episode Sister Bertrille was misidentified as an enemy aircraft and nearly shot down by the U.S. Air Force. Helping her survive all these hair-raising adventures were her friends: the convent's Mother Superior (played by Madeleine Sherwood), the wise and affectionate Sister Jacqueline (Marge Redmond), the Spanish-speaking Sister Sixto (Shelley Morrison), who constantly butchered the English language, and Carlos Ramirez (Alejandro Rey), the playboy owner of a local discotheque.

Shortly after the show premiered, Sally turned twenty-one and Screen Gems showed their appreciation by gifting her with a midnight-blue Ferrari 330 convertible, complete with a stereo tapedeck. The studio also threw a lavish $16,000 birthday bash for her at The Factory, which was at that time the Studio 54 of Los Angeles. Sally wore a bright orange velvet mini-dress, designed by Rudi Gernreich, and her escort for the evening was Davy Jones of the Monkees. They danced till all hours of the night, while photographers cheerfully snapped away and stars from other ABC and Screen Gems shows kept arriving to toast Sally's big blowout. She even had her first legal drink—Kahlua and cream. At times Sally felt like pinching herself to make sure it was all real; she wasn't used to being the center of so much attention. "I was in shock that night," she recalls. "People like Elizabeth Montgomery and Barbara Parkins were coming over to wish me happy birthday."

But that evening was one of the few times Sally actually felt part of the Hollywood community. Mainly, working on "The Flying Nun" was a lonely experience for her. She felt isolated from people her own age, trapped inside Sister Bertrille's spotless white nun's habit while the rest of her generation was wearing beads and sandals and experimenting with drugs. She was out of place, and out of touch, with the Sixties. At parties nobody bothered to talk to her—who'd want to discuss politics or crack a dirty joke in front of The Flying Nun?—and she'd wind up standing alone in a corner. After a while, she simply stopped going. "I was ostracized," she told interviewer Celeste Fremon. "Everybody was into dope and granola and saw me as part of what they were fighting against."

Away from the set, she had no real friends except for her longtime steady, Steve Craig. At night she would come home to her dark, unfurnished apartment in Malibu. She had no one to discuss the pressures of her work with—no way to let out all the anger and frustration bottled up inside her. Despite her TV success, it was definitely the darkest time in her life, and Sally may have even been on the road to borderline bulimia at this point. According to a report by journalist Elizabeth Kaye, when Sally came home from a hard day at the studio, "she would make spaghetti and bake chocolate cakes, eat everything, then try to throw up in the sink." Afterwards, she'd lie on her bare living room floor and listen to Dionne Warwick singing "The Theme From Valley of the Dolls" and cry herself to sleep.

Her only release during this time was her apprenticeship at the Actors Studio. Sensing that Sally was depressed about her career and her life in general, Madeleine Sherwood, who was a member of the prestigious "Method" acting group, had suggested that Sally join, too. Attending classes there several nights a week quickly became her salvation. People like Jack Nicholson, Ellen Burstyn, and Sally Kellerman were among Lee Strasberg's prize students, and Sally became determined to earn the master's approval, too. She idolized him, and when Strasberg rated her performance in a workshop production of Sartre's The Respectful Prostitute as "brilliant," Sally was ecstatic. Strasberg was validating what she'd always believed deep down inside: that she was cut out for more formidable roles than Gidget and The Flying Nun. "I was just a little situation-comedy heroine by day," she said, "but at night at the Actors Studio I was learning to get in touch with my true self. I was evolving into a real actress."

During this time, she was also distancing herself from Jock's influence, and her mother's, and attempting to assert her independence—moving out of her parents' home was only one aspect of that. But she still found it difficult to make decisions about anything without consulting her mother first. She had no real friends except her mother and her sister, so who else was there to ask?

The Malibu apartment stayed unfurnished because Sally was afraid to decorate it. She was afraid to spend any of the money she was now earning. She was petrified that "The Flying Nun" might be canceled tomorrow and she had nightmares of never working again. Her miserliness, unreasonable as it might have seemed, was deeply embedded in her nature, and all tangled up with the financial and emotional turbulence of her childhood. No matter how successful she became, she couldn't bring herself to live like a star—or even to dress like one. She never went on lavish vacations, or treated herself to furs or jewelry. All her clothes were bargain-basement and local thrift-shop purchases. It was common knowledge that the production secretaries at Screen Gems dressed better than Sally did.

In the midst of her confusion and loneliness, the one constant in her life was Steve Craig. After graduating from USC, he'd decided not to go on to medical school (it had dawned on him that his mother and his teachers wanted him to be a doctor more than he did) and had switched career goals. He was now taking post-graduate courses at UCLA and thinking about becoming a writer. The more Sally drew apart from her mother, who'd always been her number-one confidante, the more she turned to Steve. She simply wasn't strong enough to stand on her own yet. If she had been, she might not have rushed into marriage when she did.

In 1968—when Sally was almost twenty-two and Steve was twenty-four—they eloped to Las Vegas. According to one journalist, their marriage was more like "a legalized friendship" than a mature relationship, but for the first few years at least, Steve's affection and support were the most positive forces in Sally's life. By her own admission, Sally's defenses were as solid and unyielding as "the Great Wall of China"—Steve was the only person who could ever really chip away at that wall. She told *Redbook*'s Aimee Lee Ball that she didn't have a single real friend, outside of her family, till she met him. "I really let him in, in all the places in my soul," she said. Whenever Sally's "China Wall" would go up, Steve was endlessly patient. He always knew how to tease her out of her funk. He'd bring her flowers, joke around with her, and if that didn't work, he'd grab her by the shoulders and shake her till she'd break down and tell him what was troubling her. He refused to let her shut him out!

That had been the pattern between them for eight years. By the time Steve and Sally got married, there were few secrets between them. Neither went into the relationship with blinders on—they knew each other far better than most couples who tie the knot and, at the beginning at least, their mutual honesty seemed to give them a definite edge at the newlywed game.

But each of them was carrying a bit of excess baggage, too. Steve's writing career remained nebulous and uncertain. Sally's stint on "The Flying Nun" was increasingly demoralizing to her from an artistic standpoint. Eventually, both of those factors would have a strong bearing on the marriage.

Early in 1969, while filming the third and final season of "The Flying Nun," Sally became pregnant. It proved to be the most unbearable humiliation yet. Considering Sister Bertrille's religious status, there was no way that Sally's condition could even be hinted at on the air, so the wardrobe department had to go to extraordinary lengths to camouflage Sally's rapidly expanding waistline. Working while pregnant was cumbersome and uncomfortable, yet Sally was contractually bound to finish the season. "It should have been the most treasured time in my life," she later said, "but there I was worrying about how tight I should pull the belt on my nun's habit." Her son Peter was born on November 10, 1969, just four days after Sally's twenty-third birthday. Screen Gems gave her a few weeks' maternity leave, then Sally returned to work to complete her last episodes of "The Flying Nun."

The show aired for the last time on September 18, 1970, although, like "Gidget," it went on to become a staple on the TV rerun circuit. After the wrap party, the cast scattered in different directions. Madeleine Sherwood returned to New York and the Broadway stage. She also appeared periodically on the daytime soaps, including a stint as Betty Eiler on "The Guiding Light." Alejandro Rey also drifted into soap roles. In 1976 he played Karl Duval, one of Susan Hayes's innumerable lovers, on "Days of Our Lives"; and in 1984 he appeared briefly on "Santa Barbara" as Dr. Ramirez (no relation to Carlos Ramirez of old San Juan). Of all the "Flying Nun" graduates, aside from Sally Field, Marge Redmond has actually remained the most visible: She became a household name as Sara Tucker of Tucker's Inn in the long-running Cool Whip commercial.

Once Sally shed her coronet and habit, she decided to concentrate on made-for-television movies, which would allow her more time at home with her infant son than a weekly series. In quick succession, she starred in *Maybe I'll Come Home in the Spring* (1970), *Marriage Year One* (1971), and *Hitched* (1971). *Hitched* and *Marriage Year One* both had a romantic newlywed theme, but *Maybe I'll Come Home in the Spring* attempted to deal with more serious subject matter. Sally played a young woman who leaves home and joins a commune. She eventually gets disillusioned and returns home after a shattering drug experience. Her supporting cast included her former Screen Gems boss, Jackie Cooper, Eleanor Parker, Ed Lauter, and David Carradine.

On May 15, 1972, Steve and Sally became parents of a second son, Elijah, and eight months later she was offered yet a third television series, a frothy comedy called "The Girl With Something Extra." This time Sally would have a husband (John Davidson), a wisecracking best friend (Zohra Lampert), and something a little out of the suburban norm—powers of E.S.P. The comedy would revolve around the fact that Sally's character could read everybody else's mind. Gone were her dreams of taking up where Carole Lombard and Katharine Hepburn had left off, it seemed. This was certainly a far cry from Lee Strasberg's classes—not to mention Shakespeare and Chekhov country.

Sally was loath to return to the captivity of weekly television, but financial considerations had to take precedence. Everyone, including Steve (whom she was basically supporting—his writing career was still getting off the ground), urged her to lower her sights a little and take the show. Besides, the movies weren't exactly banging down her door. So she gave in and did the sensible thing, as she'd always done.

But this time Sally was in for a rude awakening. "The Girl With Something Extra"—positioned right after "Sanford & Son" on NBC's Friday-night line-up—barely limped through the season, and was not renewed. There were several factors involved: "The Odd Couple," which aired on ABC opposite Sally's show, was a solid ratings hit; and something was definitely missing in Sally's on-screen relationship with John Davidson. They had more than enough dimples between them, but their chemistry was uninspired. Or maybe they were just too cute at a time when TV was veering sharply away from the Rob and Laura Petrie couple-style that Mary Tyler Moore and Dick Van Dyke made famous. On shows like "Maude" and "All in the Family," comedy with a bite was now the rage. Even Mary Tyler Moore was dabbling in dark humor on her top-rated sitcom about life in a Minneapolis newsroom.

At the age of twenty-seven, Sally Field was beginning to feel too many doors were already closed to her. She had no movie career, and after "The Girl With Something Extra," she was no longer the girl with the Midas touch, as far as the TV studios were concerned. She was angry at her husband for pushing her to do the show in the first place, and she was angry at herself for giving in.

She was also cut off from her mentor, Lee Strasberg, and whether she recognized it or not, her rift with Strasberg had left a serious void in her professional life. Sally always seemed to gravitate toward strong men. When she was a girl, her stepfather, Jock Mahoney, had dominated her life; later on, Martin Ritt, who directed her in *Norma Rae* and *Back Roads,* would become her most enduring mentor and father-figure. But in the early 1970s Sally still revered Strasberg as an oracle of acting and actors' needs. His approval was crucial to her, and without it, she seemed to drift on a sea of indecision professionally.

The rift had occurred in 1970, right after "The Flying Nun" went off the air. For two years Strasberg had been showering Sally with praise—referring to her as one of his most brilliant students—but on one occasion he criticized her, unexpectedly and scathingly, after she finished doing a scene in class. In front of the other students, he called her a "coward" for choosing the easy way out in doing the scene, for not being more honest in her emotions. Sally was humiliated and never went back to class.

Years later, she realized that Strasberg's criticism hadn't been arbitrary and sadistic, after all. He was trying to get her to dig deeper in her acting than she was willing to do. The glib responses that worked for her on TV weren't enough. She was capable of expressing so much more. "I was showing off," Sally recalled. "And Lee was saying, 'You have to stop acting and start behaving. You have to go to the pain.' And I wasn't willing to do that yet."

She eventually wrote to Strasberg, acknowledging that she finally understood the message that he'd been trying to hammer home to her, but she never returned to the Actors Studio. By 1973 so many ties in her life were beginning to come apart—not only her connection with the Actors Studio, but her pattern of drifting from one situation-comedy show to another.

She was putting her TV life behind her, and, in more than one sense, the last vestiges of her girlhood, too. The next connection to come unraveled would be her marriage.

4. In the Land of Doom

"The Girl With Something Extra" aired for the last time on May 14, 1974, and after its demise, Sally went into a tailspin. The first wall that came tumbling down was her marriage.

Things on the home front had been steadily going from bad to worse for some time. For starters, Sally was unhappy with their extravagant, showcase house in Bel-Air, which Steve had urged her to buy and which they'd just spent a year redecorating. The Bel-Air house may have looked like a layout right out of *Architectural Digest*—all glass and raw wood and polished sea stone—but as far as Sally was concerned, the place was an albatross, an overpriced symbol of everything that was wrong with her life. It might as well have been made of twigs and straw. She wanted out. Out of the house. Out of the marriage. Out of the claustrophic sense of not being in control of her life.

She fired her agent, fired her manager, and fired her husband—i.e., asked him for a divorce—practically in one fell swoop. Then Sally scooped up her kids and moved into a nondescript little tract house in a small community north of

Malibu. It was located in the middle of nowhere and called, appropriately enough, Point Doom.

The fateful confrontation with Steve had been brewing for some time, but when it finally occurred, it came—as such things often do—not with a bang but a whimper. It happened one afternoon while Sally was preparing lunch; to be precise, she was heating up a can of Campbell's tomato soup. Suddenly, something inside her snapped, and she realized she had to escape. She couldn't stand to be married, not for another single moment. In the midst of her realization, lunch wound up everywhere—except on the kitchen table.

She was forcing herself, for the first time, to look at her situation honestly. And what did she see? Where was the golden life that she and Steve had supposedly been living? It had started coming apart at the seams long ago. By this time their "fairy-tale marriage" was just a lie—nine-tenths public pretense and one-tenth wishful thinking. It existed only in the fanciful embroidery of gossip columns and fan magazines. And Sally was tired of playing a role that belied her deepest feelings—and unable to control her anger anymore. Standing there in the kitchen, she picked up the open can of soup and hurled it across the room. It splattered all over the kitchen walls and ceiling. Then, she quietly went into the next room and asked Steve for a divorce. Sally later remarked, "I was going down for the count." She sincerely believed that if she hadn't done something drastic right then and there, she might have lost her mind or turned into an "alcoholic housewife."

What had gone wrong? Sally was obviously bitter over the cancellation of "The Girl With Something Extra," and she blamed Steve for pushing her into the project in the first place. Later, Sally also spoke of basic differences in their natures that had gradually driven them apart. Apparently, they were a classic case of opposites attracting and then being unable to meet each other halfway.

Steve, the free spirit, and Sally, the play-it-by-the-book traditionalist, certainly knew how to bring out the best (and the worst) in each other. It was a San Fernando Valley variation on *The Catcher in the Rye*: Gidget Lawrence had gone suburban with Holden Caulfield. Steve was easygoing and unconcerned about his appearance. Sally was neat and very structured. He was a "social renegade," as she once put it, while she was born to look both ways before crossing the street. If a door said OUT, Steve would purposely swing it open and try to bulldoze his way through, just to flout authority. "He became a man who could not live within society's rules," Sally explained to *Redbook*'s Aimee Lee Ball. And, as a result of his hang-loose attitude, other doors stayed shut, too. More and more, Sally balked at the fact that Steve rarely worked. "He spent most of his time going to college, where he felt safe," she said. "And I spent most of my time working and supporting him. Slowly I began to resent that."

Still and all, the divorce was extremely painful, maybe because it wasn't the kind that made flamboyant headlines. There wasn't another woman involved. Or another man. Or a drinking problem. Or cruelty or abandonment. In a strange way, those things might have made the dissolution easier to face. No, this was the breakup of two decent, caring people who had been very close for a very long time. And that kind of failure hurt a great deal on both sides. Steve Craig had been the only man in Sally's life—at times her only friend—ever since she was fourteen. In a sense, leaving him meant leaving behind her childhood, literally cutting off a part of her life. For in spite of everything, there was no denying one bittersweet fact: Sally still cared for him. "I still love him . . . with every part of my being," she said. Yet she had to tell him, "I can't live this way."

And so the divorce went through. Sally Field, the former girl-next-door, became Sally Field, sole breadwinner and single parent. A new chapter in her life was beginning.

Priorities had to change now. After Sally and her sons got settled out at Point Doom, the first order of business was trying to shift gears professionally. "I had to forget that I had once been a television star and I had to force myself to start over," she confided. "For once, I was damn well going to do what I really wanted—get a foothold in the movies!"

Not that she expected it to be easy. Sally fully realized that she was taking an enormous gamble with her career; in fact, she might very well be flushing it down the tubes. The motion-picture business was about as stable as the San Andreas fault line. She might get cast in the next Stanley Kubrick or John Schlesinger picture—she might also never get an acting job again and wind up slinging hash or selling door-to-door cosmetics for the rest of her life. But win, lose, or draw, for once at least, she intended to be in the driver's seat, making her own decisions.

Whether or not she actually broke into films—or merely broke her back trying—Sally promised herself one thing: Never again would she "work in a shallow series," typecast as "the cute, glib girl-next-door."

Professionally, she made a complete break with the past and forced herself to abandon old habits, old support-systems, old ruts. For starters, she enrolled in a musical-comedy acting class, run by Nancy Walker's husband, David Craig. Not that Sally was the least bit interested in becoming the next Barbra Streisand or Bernadette Peters. She signed up for it simply because Craig's workshop was known as the toughest acting class in Los Angeles—and Sally knew it was time to scare herself good and hard. She needed to take on the hardest challenge she could find. Her singing, quite frankly, was no match for her enthusiasm, but she persevered. Every week Craig told her she was bloody awful, but sugar-coated his evaluation a little by reminding her how courageous she was for trying so hard. Those left-handed compliments were all that sustained her through the very bleak year of 1974.

And professionally it was undoubtedly the bleakest year of her life to date. Sally kept going on movie auditions for parts she never got; at the same time, TV producers kept offering her roles in embarrassingly bad new series that all read like recycled rip-offs of "Gidget" and "The Flying Nun." Sally joked that one producer wanted her to play "The Galloping Gourmiss," a Julia Child on wings who flew around the country whipping up fabulous *flambées* for clients who depended on her culinary efforts and cookbook psychology. You see, Sally not only pulled their buns out of the oven, she also saved marriages, retrieved friendships, and reunited lost collies with their tearful owners.

Sally decided she'd rather starve than do trash like that. And for a time it indeed looked like Sally and her kids might be passing up prime rib for Spam sandwiches and peanut butter—permanently.

Then, in 1975, opportunity knocked: Bob Rafelson, the director who'd scored a major triumph with the 1970 Jack Nicholson film, *Five Easy Pieces,* suddenly came into Sally's life. He was looking for an actress to play Jeff Bridges's and Arnold Schwarzenegger's leading lady in his new film, *Stay Hungry.* The part—an earthy health-spa receptionist with a sexy Southern drawl—was about a million light-years away from anything Sally had ever done before. Certainly, she wasn't on Rafelson's A-list of contenders for the part. But that didn't intimidate her in the least. Sally got wind of the part from Zohra Lampert, her former castmate on "The Girl With Something Extra," and Lampert recommended her to Rafelson's office. The casting director, who took the call from Sally's agent, was shocked that Sally Field even wanted to be considered for such an "adult" role. The language was raunchy, the wardrobe was skimpy, there was even a nude scene involved. "Sally Field? Are you kidding?" he gasped. But Sally's agent pushed, pestered, and pleaded until the casting director finally agreed to set up an interview.

Bob Rafelson had his doubts, too. Despite the strength of her audition, he had Sally come back for reading after reading because he couldn't quite dissociate her from "The Flying Nun." Meanwhile, Sally became so desperate that she overprepared to the point of ridiculousness. After so many rejections in the last year, she was obsessed about getting this particular part. Even when she wasn't auditioning, she stayed in character twenty-four hours a day, walking around the house spouting obscenities like the girl she was hoping to portray in *Stay Hungry*. Even her children thought her behavior was rather strange. "Mom's swearing like a truck-driver again," they said, but it didn't really faze them. By this time, they were used to the fact that Mom was a Method actress.

Sally may not have looked the part, but she had one thing going for her—her fiery temperament. For the first time, Sally found a way to express her anger through her performance—and it helped her land the role. "I put all my anger into the acting," she revealed in a *McCall's* interview. "When I read, I was so intense that there was a *volcano* in the room." After six readings, the part was finally hers.

Aside from the fact that *Stay Hungry* helped Sally make

the transition from TV to film, it remains memorable for another reason—it contains her first and, until recently, only nude scene. Would she have agreed to do that scene if her film career had been on a firmer footing? That's something we'll never know. Certainly, it doesn't quite jibe with the later image we have of Sally as the star of *Absence of Malice* and *Places in the Heart*—films that were serious but subdued. At any rate, one thing is certain: From start to finish, Sally was extremely uncomfortable disrobing for the camera in *Stay Hungry*.

To make things easier, Rafelson gave her a choice: She could rehearse the scene with her clothes on or off. If she decided to rehearse with her clothes on, she'd only have to appear naked in front of the camera (and the crew) once—for the final take. But Sally—ever the Method actress—volunteered to remove her robe during rehearsal. She felt if she waited until filming to drop the robe, she wouldn't have time to feel comfortable with her nakedness on the set. She wouldn't know what to do with her hands, or how to stand or move around. She worried that she'd end up looking like a walking zombie—a statue with goosebumps—in the scene.

Rafelson cleared the set, except for eight crew members whose presence was absolutely necessary. The scene itself was brief: All Sally had to do was walk across the room, just a few yards, and get into bed with Jeff Bridges. But she wound up walking miles and miles that day because she couldn't get it right. In her nervousness, she kept screwing things up. Getting the right camera shot was a delicate proposition. In order to make sure there was no frontal nudity, Sally was required to walk a very narrow line so that the camera caught her only from an oblique angle. The minute she veered even an inch or two to the left or right, the shot became X-rated and unusable. In take after take Sally got it wrong, and that merciless walk across the room—in front of Jeff Bridges, Rafelson, and the eight technicians—had to be repeated. It became interminable.

As the rehearsals dragged on, the situation became more and more humiliating for Sally. The cameramen—who cared only about reframing the damn shot and getting it done—were virtually oblivious to Sally's presence and certainly insensitive to her feelings. They discussed her body as if they were talking about an inanimate prop or a piece of uncooperative scenery. "No, we can't use that shot because her pubic hair is showing," they'd say, or "She's ruining it with too much crotch."

"It was the most awful feeling in the world," Sally recalls. "I felt as if I were being X-rayed and examined from head to foot, as if someone had pulled my pants down in public and everyone in the world could see me!"

Sally, however, was so grateful to be working on the film that she didn't want to do anything to upset the apple cart. So she bit her lip and swallowed her indignation. After about a dozen takes, however, Jeff Bridges could see that she was barely holding back tears and on the verge of losing control. During a break he came over and asked what was wrong. When Sally told him, she broke down and cried. At that point, she felt she simply wasn't tough-skinned enough to get through the scene—she was too shaky and embarrassed to go on—and she was petrified that Rafelson was going to fire her. She couldn't even make that walk across the bedroom without trembling all over. Bridges urged her to talk to Rafelson, but she was afraid to approach him alone, so they went together. Surprisingly enough, Rafelson was more sympathetic than Sally had expected him to be. If he'd known to begin with how uncomfortable she felt, he never would have let her do all those rehearsals in the buff, he said. After his talk with her, Rafelson went back and ordered the crew to treat her with kid gloves because she was having a hard time with the scene. As soon as the rough edges of the situation were smoothed down, Sally relaxed and the next take was a wrap.

Sally never forgot the kindness of Jeff Bridges, her on-the-set rescuer that day. She considered him one of the most thoughtful, sensitive men she'd ever met, and as a result of *Stay Hungry,* Jeff became a permanent friend. Four years later, she worked with his brother, Beau, in *Norma Rae,* and in 1982 she and Jeff were reunited on-screen in the romantic comedy *Kiss Me Goodbye.*

Although the film didn't set any records at the box office, *Stay Hungry* accomplished two things for Sally Field's career: It proved to Hollywood that she was a serious dramatic actress, and it took a lot of the starch out of her stodgy Flying Nun image by spotlighting her in a role that was both sexy and vulgar. Movie critic Gene Siskel praised her performance and noted that "walking around the film's gym in a leotard, she startled many viewers with her sex appeal."

Nevertheless, movie offers didn't start pouring in as a result of her stunning success in *Stay Hungry.* The irony of it was that just when Hollywood was finally beginning to recognize Sally's talent, there weren't enough women's roles around worth fighting for. In the mid-1970s American movies had reached a low point as far as female casting was concerned. Except for Barbra Streisand, there was no actress who could guarantee box-office success. The movies, it seemed, were having a love affair with men. Stars like Robert Redford, Al Pacino, and Jack Nicholson were making films with buddy co-stars instead of beautiful leading ladies, while Jane Fonda and Faye Dunaway scrambled for whatever roles were left over. In 1975, the same year that Sally Field made *Stay Hungry,* so few actresses had scored major film triumphs that the Academy of Motion Picture Arts and Sciences had a hard time nominating five women in the Best Actress category. Louise Fletcher (hardly a major star) ultimately won the Oscar for *One Flew Over the Cuckoo's Nest,* but it was hardly a knock-down drag-out contest—her biggest competitor was Ann-Margret for *Tommy,* Ken Russell's Technicolor rock opera.

Not only were there few screen roles for women, there were even fewer roles for conventional, cute-looking, all-American types. The Seventies were significant for the glorification of the "outsider" on the silver screen—ethnic types like Talia Shire, kooky types like Diane Keaton, and cerebral types like Glenda Jackson and Ellen Burstyn were the dominant figures of the decade. Even if Sally Field had been able to elbow her way into more directors' offices, it's difficult to imagine what part Francis Ford Coppola would have offered her in *The Godfather,* or John Avildsen would have handpicked her for in *Rocky.*

So mainly Sally Field stayed home. She spent time with her children, worked on her garden, and started remodeling her house. She ripped up old carpets and stripped floors down to the bare wood. The physical labor actually became therapeutic. It made her feel that even if she never worked in movies again, she could survive. And at the same time, she cultivated her first relationship since the breakup of her marriage. In April 1976, *New York Post* columnist Earl Wilson reported that Sally was "living in an unmarried state with Coulter Adams," who'd been the assistant director on *Stay Hungry.*

Sally didn't deny the arrangement. "I'm living with somebody I love and I'm happy to do it," she said. "I'm not casual. I'm seriously in love with this man." It seemed like a comfortable enough setup. Adams, who was three years younger than Sally, got along well with her sons, Peter and Elijah, and Sally's ex, Steve Craig, had no objections. Certainly he had no reason to worry about Adams trying to replace him as a father-figure in the house. Steve lived nearby and saw the boys often; he and Sally had worked out a loose, flexible visitation arrangement, and since the divorce they had actually been getting on much better than they had while they were married.

Sally's main problem now was finding the next step up the creative ladder. It was more than a year since she had made *Stay Hungry,* and she was still up to her ears in sawdust instead of scripts. But when she was half-done remodeling the porch, a part came along that made all the waiting worthwhile. The project was called *Sybil.*

Sally was cast as the lead, and the part promised to challenge her more than any role she had ever played. *Sybil* was scheduled to be an NBC-TV movie during the 1976–77 season. It was based on the best-selling true account of a woman suffering from a multiple-personality disorder who manifests sixteen separate identities. Joanne Woodward was set to play the sympathetic psychiatrist who befriends Sybil and eventually helps her exorcise her demons. (The casting of Woodward as the psychiatrist, rather than the schizophrenic, was a significant event in itself, for it gave her the chance to play the other side of the coin: In 1957 Woodward won an Oscar for her unforgettable portrayal of a Sybil-like character, though with only a trio of personalities, in *The Three Faces of Eve.*)

Until now Sally had been adamant about not returning to television, but her fascination with the role of Sybil far outweighed her opposition. *Sybil* would surely be a once-in-alifetime experience, for she'd be playing not one but sixteen different characters. The movie was scheduled to run as part of NBC's "Big Event," a new catch-all phrase for Sunday-night music and dramatic specials on the network. "Big Events" included everything from movies like *Gone With the Wind* to brand-new, big-budget mini-series like Kirk Douglas's *The Moneychangers*.

Working on *Sybil* proved to be more physically and emotionally draining than anything Sally had ever tackled. By her own admission, "I was in a state of near-hysteria all the time," and when she came home from the studio at night she was literally too exhausted to cook dinner or take care of the children. Her mother basically moved in and took over. All Sally wanted to do when she came home was fall into bed and sleep. The TV-movie took its toll in other ways, too. She began to suffer from bad dreams and was often unaccountably depressed. Getting into Sybil's skin might have been more than Sally had bargained for.

Adding to everything else was Sally's worry that her energy would give out in midstream and she wouldn't be able to complete the project. Two weeks into rehearsal, though, things improved considerably when the original director was fired and replaced by Dan Petrie, who had a reputation for quality work. At that point, cast spirit had hit rock-bottom. Everyone had begun to feel weighed down by the enormity of the project they'd undertaken—trying to make a coherent, interesting drama out of material that was both clinical and complex. But under Petrie's guidance, things began improving at once. The script was tightened and humanized; the actors began to relate to their roles, and rehearsals became stimulating rather than exhausting. Sally found herself feeling less tired—and more enthusiastic—as the project gained momentum.

Sally's one major conflict with the producers arose over the question of wardrobe. Originally, each of her sixteen different personalities was supposed to have a different wardrobe, but Sally refused to make the costume changes. She felt the producers were trying to glamorize the role for the sake of ratings and sacrificing dramatic reality in the process. Sybil wasn't rich enough to afford all those clothes, she argued, and eventually won her point.

During the course of the film, Sally had to exhibit extreme anger, fear, violence, sexuality, and hysteria. None of her many moments on-screen was particularly easy, but the true test of her talent came during a sixteen-page scene where Sally had to change into five different personalities in rapid succession. "It was the hardest piece of acting I've ever had to do—harder even than anything that came later in *Norma Rae* or my other movies," she conceded. When Sally wrapped that scene, Joanne Woodward turned to her and said, "Wow! Next to this, *The Three Faces of Eve* was a piece of cake!"

On September 12, 1977, Hollywood rewarded Sally with an Emmy as Best Actress in a Comedy or Drama Special. The program itself was voted Outstanding Special of the Year, tying with another tele-movie, *Eleanor and Franklin: The White House Years*. Although victory was sweet (it was the first citation she ever received for serious dramatic acting), the moment was tempered somewhat by the fact that Sally did not attend the awards ceremonies. She knew the competition was stiff, and she wanted to win so much that she wasn't sure she could keep her emotions in check. To be perfectly blunt about it, she was worried about coming off as a sore loser. She was afraid that if someone else's name was read when the magic envelope was opened, she might not be cordial to the winner.

That November Sally celebrated her thirty-first birthday. With her Emmy for *Sybil* prominently displayed in her living room, Sally could finally feel that she was starting to make strides in the business. She could take pride in the fact that she was being recognized and accepted as an actress who was more than just an "economy-size Doris Day" (as one reviewer had once dubbed her). But, on the personal side, there were still a few blank spaces waiting to be filled in. Peter was eight now; Eli was five. Her sons were the one bright spot in an otherwise unsettled personal life. Her relationship with Coulter Adams was long over, and while there was an actor named Burt Reynolds on the horizon, right from the beginning there was a part of herself that Sally held back. Reynolds, she sensed, was the ultimate charmer, but not really the marrying kind. His highly publicized romances with Hollywood's most beautiful women were ample proof of that.

So where was that proverbial Mr. Right? Knights in shining armor were in short supply. All the most fascinating men, it seemed, were already taken, or not much interested in long-term relationships, or not much interested in women, period. What Sally truly wanted, she realized, was to be married. "I'm one of the world's great wives," she said. "I'm a wife in search of a home."

5. Plumbing, Parenting . . .
And a Phone Call From Burt

"I'm a mother before anything else . . . I'm committed to my children," Sally frequently reminds interviewers. "I cook, I make jam, I make quilts. I'm really very much a homebody."

In 1980, when she won her first Academy Award for *Norma Rae,* she put it another way. In her acceptance speech, Sally said, "Without my kids, I'm not worth a damn."

However, child-rearing hasn't always been easy for Sally. She was a single parent for a long time (she didn't remarry until 1984) and she's been a working mother all of the boys' lives. When her sons were small and Sally first started getting movie work, she hired a housekeeper to take care of them. At times when she was on location in Texas or Florida, her mother would move in temporarily to supervise things in Sally's absence.

Undoubtedly, Sally's highs and lows have affected both her sons. Eli was born when she was finishing up "The Flying Nun." It was a time in her life when she felt angry and stifled—angry at being stuck in television, at having to be the family breadwinner, at not being able to pursue her real dreams. Her sense of frustration, she concedes, definitely played a part in molding Eli's personality. He slept fitfully at night until he was eight months old.

Sally couldn't cope with his cranky behavior. One night in exasperation she threw him down on the bed, not to hurt him, just to frighten him enough so he would stop crying, but she still carries the guilt of losing her temper that one time. She later confided to *Ladies' Home Journal* writer Eleanor Stukane that she felt her anger had left permanent emotional scars on her son. Soon after that incident, he started "to hold his breath and have epileptic-type fits. His body would go into spasm, his back would arch, and his face would become grotesque and turn blue."

Sally realized these seizures were Eli's way of fighting back, but she felt powerless to deal with his behavior. She didn't send him to nursery school or let anyone take care of him when she was away, except his father. (Even today Steve and Eli are especially close.) Magically, the seizures stopped when Eli was three and a half. Sally reasons that perhaps he was old enough then to verbalize his anger, and no longer had to resort to physical extremes to make himself heard. But even today Sally concedes that Eli still has a pretty hot temper.

Of the two, Peter has always seemed more likely to gravitate toward show business. From the time he was very young, he was extremely interested in his mother's career and occasionally would even read her scripts. Both boys, though, were unimpressed by their mother's television series. Peter once told her flat out that he "thought 'The Flying Nun' was crap," and he and Eli never bothered to catch her old shows in rerun. That stuff was just too boring. There's one other performance they never caught—her work in

Sybil. Sally was afraid that her bizarre and frightening character changes in the film might traumatize them too much.

By the time she made *Norma Rae,* Peter was ten and Eli was seven, so she was able to prepare them for some of the dramatic clashes that they'd see her engaged in on-screen. Every day Sally would come home from the studio and tell the boys a little bit more of the story, so that when they saw the film, they'd be comfortable with the story and nothing would shock them. Nevertheless, the film was so emotionally overpowering that at one point Peter broke down and cried. It was the scene where Norma Rae sits down with her kids and tells them the sordid truth about herself, the mistakes she's made and the trouble she's been in.

Most of the time, though, Sally tried to keep her kids as uninvolved with her career as possible. At home with her family, away from the glaring lights of the studio and the glittering hype of publicity, Sally tried her darndest to be just an ordinary parent. She disciplined her kids, called them every night when she was on the road, and brought them lavish presents, admittedly out of guilt, when she returned. She claimed she was much stricter than her ex-husband when it came to keeping the boys in line. "I'm the one who lays down the law," she's often said. "When they're at their father's house, it's one huge vacation."

She told *Us* magazine, "The reality of my life has nothing to do with Hollywood or glamor. Reality for me is: The kids are late for school, the cat ate their homework, the window is broken, the toilet is stopped up." Sally frequently swore that if she ever married again, she'd find a guy who had mastered the intricacies of indoor plumbing. She didn't care if he drove a Mercedes or a Ford pickup truck—as long as he knew a wrench from a screwdriver!

Without a man around the house, the boys often pitched in to help their mother handle whatever needed unjamming or unclogging. Once they tried to help her paint the living room. "The paint wound up everywhere, except on the walls," laughed Sally, "but what the hell—we had fun!"

Sometimes when her mother came over to cook, clean, and take care of the kids, the topsy-turvey quality of the household situation began to get to Sally. She had the strange feeling that Grandma was the mommy in the house and she herself, who marched off to work every morning and didn't come home till late at night, had turned into the daddy. As the boys grew older, Sally felt the lack of a male presence in the house even more sharply. "My boys and I feed on each other. We give each other strength," Sally insisted, but at times she wondered how her sons felt living in a house where all the decisions—about work, money, school, everything—were being made by a woman. "Well, all I can do is try to feel good about myself as a woman, and not be ashamed or try to apologize," she said.

There were days, of course, when Sally felt both incredibly sad, and angry at herself, for the time her career took away from her family. "How selfish I am," she thought. "Why can't I be satisfied just staying home and being a mother?" Originally, she had no choice about working—she had to put food on the table. But even if her financial situation had been otherwise, Sally still would have pursued a career. Acting had been the motivating force in her life, the obsession that shaped everything, for as long as she could remember.

But once the boys were in school, she felt the lack of a man around the house more keenly. Her sons were growing up and they needed a father who'd be there on a daily basis, not just on holidays and weekends. Sally herself needed someone permanent, too. Her life was consumed, it seemed, by motherhood and work, but neither of those enterprises was enough to keep her from being lonely.

Perhaps Sally didn't even realize just how lonely she was until Burt Reynolds came along. His arrival changed everything.

Sally was cast as Sybil in April 1976, and a few weeks after shooting ended, her agent brought her a strange message. Burt Reynolds had phoned. He wanted Sally as his leading lady in his next film, *Smokey and the Bandit*. If the Prince of Wales had phoned, Sally couldn't have been more surprised or more mystified.

Actually, it was Hal Needham, Burt's longtime friend and the director of the film, who had first suggested Sally's name. But Burt was immediately fascinated by the notion, not that he had any idea at all if Sally could pull her own weight in a movie. He hadn't bothered to see *Stay Hungry*, and *Sybil* was still in an NBC editing room, but none of that mattered. Burt wanted her because he thought she was a great comedienne. He'd been a big fan of "Gidget" and "The Flying Nun."

Burt also sensed that he and Sally were kindred spirits of a sort. Sally was still trying to live down her eternal cheerleader image. He was fighting tooth-and-nail to make people forget that he'd ever posed nude for *Cosmopolitan* magazine. Burt didn't think Hollywood gave Sally enough credit for the caliber of work she'd done in her three TV series. "It was actually real good television she was doing back then," he told writer Elizabeth Kaye. "It was a joke at the time—this person flying around with a habit on. But she made it work. The mere fact that it had stayed on the air so long is an incredible tribute to her as an actress. But it's easy to make jokes about nuns. Just like it's easy to do a centerfold joke. I identified with that."

Professionally, Burt felt nearly as trapped in a stereotypical straitjacket as Sally did. He'd been trying to prove that he was more than just a handsome hunk ever since his college football days in Florida. His first assault on Hollywood didn't stop traffic. In 1959 he got his start as Darren McGavin's co-star in the TV-western series "Riverboat," then he played Quint Asper, a half-breed Indian blacksmith, on "Gunsmoke" for three seasons. In 1966 Burt traded in his buckskins for a leather jacket and starred in his first cops-and-robbers series, a show called "Hawk." This time he played an Iroquois Indian turned New York City police officer who hunted down criminals from Park Avenue to Harlem. The show died after half a season. Four years later Burt headlined in another shoot-'em-up series, "Dan August," where he was cast as a California police detective. That show also faded out after a short run.

Ironically, what made Burt Reynolds a star wasn't episodic television, nor his early movies. It was his 1972 bare-bottomed romp on the pages of *Cosmopolitan.* Burt was the first male celebrity to pose for the centerfold of a national magazine, and the issue sold like hot cakes. In two days, two and a half million copies of that infamous April 1972 issue were snatched off the newsstand, and collectors later paid much higher prices for it. But baring all had a minus side as well as a plus. While the ploy turned Burt into an instant sex symbol, it also made the film industry refuse to take his acting career very seriously. Burt's antics were considered a tacky, outrageous publicity stunt and Hollywood regarded him with the condescending snobbery it would later reserve for Sean Penn and Pia Zadora.

Burt's greatest desire was to be recognized as a real actor;

Hollywood refused to see him as anything but a pin-up poster and a clown.

Ironically, to this day, Burt's most successful films remain his comedies. His few, spare efforts at serious drama have never elevated him into quite the same league as Robert De Niro and Dustin Hoffman. In 1972—the same year he posed nude for *Cosmopolitan*—Burt made *Deliverance,* a critically acclaimed film about four Southern businessmen whose macho male fantasies are shattered during a terrifying weekend in the wilderness. Both the film and John Boorman, the director, were nominated for Academy Awards, but Burt Reynolds's performance was passed over in the Best Actor category. Nevertheless, his comedies helped keep Universal and Warner Brothers in business all through the 1970s. *Smokey and the Bandit*—which earned over $61 million—was the second-highest grossing comedy film of the decade. *Hooper* ($37 million) and *Smokey and the Bandit II* (almost $38 million) were right up there in the top twenty.

For better or for worse, it was *Smokey and the Bandit* that brought Burt and Sally together. To put it mildly, it wasn't exactly the kind of romance that Sally's grandmother—or for that matter, anybody's grandmother—would have approved of. Burt's reputation preceded him. "Women are my drugs and alcohol," he once said. "When I'm involved with one woman, I'm involved with one woman. Period. But between romances, I am carnivorous."

And the record spoke for itself. In the early 1960s, Burt was married to comedienne Judy Carne, who later became known as the sock-it-to-me girl on "Laugh-In." The marriage fell apart when Burt lost his role on "Gunsmoke" and Judy was signed to do her first American TV series, the sitcom "The Baileys of Balboa." According to one Burt Reynolds biographer, Marc Eliot, Burt couldn't handle the competition.

The idea that his wife's career was progressing more rapidly than his own practically put him over the brink. He became seriously depressed and stayed in the house all day with the curtains closed. According to Eliot, he began fantasizing that Judy was cheating on him.

After his divorce from Carne, Burt seemed to drift from one woman to the next. For two years he lived with Miko Mayama, who appeared in the TV series "Hey, Landlord." Then came a reputed fling with Inger Stevens (shortly before her death), followed by an involvement with Lee Majors's future wife, Farrah Fawcett, and a long-running romance with Dinah Shore, who was seventeen years older than Burt.

In 1976, when Burt and Sally crossed paths, he was just putting Dinah Shore behind him.

Sally wasn't impressed with his romantic track record or with the project he was offering her. When she read the original script of *Smokey and the Bandit,* she hated it, but her agent prodded her to call Burt anyway. Actually, part of her resistance had to do with the fact that Sally was slightly terrified of Burt himself. She literally had to force herself to make that call. In her mind, Burt Reynolds was a glamorous, probably dissipated movie idol—and that frightened her. "He was the image of everything that scared me to death," she later said. When she pictured him, she thought of somebody who was the leader of his own rat pack, who traveled in Hollywood's elite inner circle, who hung out at posh parties that she only read about. He was life in the fast lane personified.

The afternoon that she made the call, Sally had been weeding in her garden. At first, she toyed with the idea of showering and dressing up before phoning—thinking it would give her more courage—then nixed it, and said to herself, "Oh, what the heck!" and dialed his number, dirty fingernails and all. Burt started charming her the minute he picked up the receiver. (Did he suspect how petrified she was or was this just his usual routine?) "Hi. This is Burt Reynolds, Star," he said.

It was the start of a beautiful—and bizarre—friendship.

It was perfect casting when Sally Field won the coveted role of TV's Gidget. Raised in Southern California, she had spent every school vacation at the beach.

As Gidget Lawrence, Sally worried about the three b's—boys, beach parties, and bikinis. Betty Conner played her protective older sister, Anne Cooper.

In 1965 Sally made a big splash in Hollywood along with "Gidget" co-stars Peter Deuel, who played her brother-in-law, John Cooper, and Lynette Winter, who played her best friend, Larue.

On the set of her first movie, The Way West, Sally gets a few pointers from director Andrew V. McLaglen (back to camera). Assistant director Terry Morse stands next to her; co-stars Richard Widmark and Michael McGreevey, both on mules, are in the background.

Sally and Michael McGreevey were cast as sweethearts in The Way West. She played the daughter of a poor white family traveling to Oregon by wagon train.

Motherhood and TV stardom isn't an easy road. In the late 1960s TV's "Flying Nun" never went anywhere without her young son, Peter, or her weekly scripts. (Pictorial Parade)

Sally's marriage to high-school classmate Steve Craig was the stuff that movie magazine fantasies are made of. Steve was her first boyfriend—and her first best friend—but their story had a bittersweet ending. (Pictorial Parade)

In 1976 Sally teamed with Jeff Bridges in the movie Stay Hungry. Through the years he remained one of her favorite leading men, and in 1982 they paired off again in Kiss Me Goodbye.

Sally became a screen bride in Smokey and the Bandit. In real life she's been to the altar twice.

During the 1970s Sally Field scored some of her finest professional triumphs. She won an Emmy for the TV movie Sybil, *and took home her first Oscar for the feature film* Norma Rae.

Dinah Shore was Sally's predecessor as Burt Reynolds's off-screen companion. Dinah was seventeen years older than Burt, but the romance was no laughing matter (even if they did share a few jokes when Burt guested on Dinah's daytime TV talk show).

Sally and Burt . . . Their romance was made in Hollywood, not heaven. Did her Oscar—and his leading ladies—eventually break them up? (Pictorial Parade)

In 1979 Sally won every major acting award for her unforgettable performance in Norma Rae, but she was outraged that her Norma Rae director, Martin Ritt (left), didn't receive an Academy Award nomination. Beau Bridges (right) played her husband in the film. (Pictorial Parade)

Back Roads (1980) cast Sally Field as a hooker and Tommy Lee Jones as a boxer, who fall in love. But their best sparring matches took place off-screen. (Pictorial Parade)

In 1981's Absence of Malice *Bob Balaban played an unscrupulous government investigator, and Sally Field was the naive reporter who becomes
involved in his dangerous schemes. (Pictorial Parade)*

Sally and a favorite escort—her younger son, Eli. (Pictorial Parade)

At a recent celebrity gala, Sally shared the spotlight with her Murphy's Romance co-star James Garner, good friend Jane Fonda, and Jane's husband, Tom Hayden. Ms. Fonda helped Ms. Field get her movie-producing career off the ground. (Pictorial Parade)

In 1985 Hollywood showed Sally "they liked her—they really liked her!" by voting her another Oscar, this time for Places in the Heart. Robert Duvall was that year's Best Actor choice for Tender Mercies. (Pictorial Parade)

Mr. and Mrs. Alan Greisman . . . The Scarsdale, New York, boy marries the San Fernando Valley girl and they both live happily ever after. (Pictorial Parade)

6. Sally and the Bandit

Sally's first phone encounter with Burt Reynolds wasn't exactly an exercise in hard Hollywood-style bargaining. She had marched over to the phone girded for battle—combat helmet securely fastened and bayonet fixed—but somehow the war she'd been anticipating just never materialized. And that threw her for a loop.

How was she supposed to cope? She'd been rehearsing her end of the conversation all afternoon, but the minute she started speaking to the suave, surprisingly humble matinee idol, all her tough talk and decisiveness went right out the window.

Burt asked if she'd read the script of *Smokey and the Bandit*. Sally said yes. Then came a long pause.

"How did you like it?" Burt wanted to know.

"Well, to be perfectly frank . . ." Sally started to tell him—launching into her carefully rehearsed harangue on a thousand and one reasons why she couldn't compromise her artistic principles and deign to make this turkey—but she never had a chance to finish. Burt—the high-powered Hollywood salesman—was already off and running, and he had a thousand and one reasons, too. He explained to her that the quality of the script really didn't matter all that much. They could fix whatever was wrong (he'd frequently made "chicken salad out of chicken shit"—those were his exact words); besides, Sally would get to travel and see "great places like Waycross, Georgia," and think of all the fun they'd have working together, and they could probably play gin rummy on the set all day because most of their scenes took place in the front seat of a car, anyway—and if none of those come-ons impressed her, just ponder this: Did she truly want to pass up the opportunity of working with the world's number-one box-office star?

Burt's outrageous combination of mock ego and dumb jokes was too much. Sally couldn't stop giggling. If this phone call was any indication of how Burt intended to behave on location, then he was absolutely right—they would have fun! Besides, she had his assurance that the script she'd just seen wasn't the script they'd actually shoot; so Sally gave in and agreed to play Carrie, the Bandit's girlfriend—CB handle, "The Frog."

Sally arrived in Atlanta on August 21, 1976, the day before filming actually began. She was barely settled in her hotel room when Burt called and invited her out for a drink that night. "I thought it was silly for us to wait and meet on the set for the first time," he recalls. "I figured we'd both be more relaxed if we got the preliminaries out of the way fast."

Sally spent the afternoon buying needlepoint patterns (so she'd have something to do on the set during rehearsal breaks), but she rushed back to her hotel room at three P.M. to start getting ready for her "date" with Burt. Even though she kept insisting to herself that Burt Reynolds was really nobody special—"just an ordinary mortal like the rest of us"—Sally was obviously a nervous wreck about meeting him. She behaved like a maniac in front of her mirror, changing from one outfit to another—trying on every piece of clothing she'd brought with her—panic-stricken over what to wear. Finally, she settled on black velvet pants and an orange Mexican shirt. Then, she was so afraid of being late that she had her makeup on and was ready and waiting for him—three hours early!

What made Sally regress into instant adolescence? The trouble was that, despite the fact that she was nearly thirty years old, hardly virginal, and the mother of two, she had no real sense of herself as a woman. She didn't think she was particularly attractive. "Up until I met Burt I only thought of myself as a good mother and a good actress," she later confessed. "Otherwise I didn't see myself in a very positive light."

Maybe that's what brought them together. Burt was the first man who really appreciated her femininity and wanted to help her cultivate it. He taught her how to dress, how to put on makeup, how to make charming small talk at parties. And Sally was a very willing Eliza Doolittle to his Professor Higgins. She was so eager to please him—at least at the beginning of their relationship—that she followed every suggestion, and ultimately every rule, he made.

In a 1986 interview with *Playboy,* Sally recalled her early days with Burt: "He gave me a feeling that I was attractive, sexy. It pleased me to dress for him. I like doing that. I like being exhibited by a man in some ways, like an object. I wanted to be the perfect person I never could be before. : . .

At first, Sally didn't know how to communicate with him. She obviously idolized Burt, but she thought he'd never be interested in the real her, so she decided she had to jazz up her personality—and become a little grittier—for him. On their first date, the night before filming began, she tried to impress him with her vulgarity and her checkered past, neither of which had existed until that moment. She simply invented a new persona on the spot! All through dinner she swore like a sailor, using the most obscene adjectives possible to discuss the food, the weather, every topic of conversation that came up. On top of that, she tried to give Burt the impression that she had dabbled with drugs and could hold her liquor with the best of them. Her performance was really quite funny. It might have been brilliant, in fact, if it hadn't been so downright pathetic.

But Burt wasn't fooled for a minute. He wasn't put off by Sally's bizarre routine, either. He sensed how uncomfortable she was. Obviously, she was putting on protective armor because she didn't want him to think of her as the Flying Nun come to life.

Unfortunately, her raunchy playacting continued right onto the set of *Smokey and the Bandit*. For the first few days of shooting, Sally referred to everything—and everyone—by four-letter words. The situation was more than embarrassing—it was almost like a page out of *Sybil*. Mature, sensible Sally Field had temporarily disappeared and a foul-mouthed guttersnipe had emerged in her place.

Finally, Burt called time out for a conference. He took Sally aside to discuss the situation. He told her in no uncertain terms that there wasn't room on the set for two Sally Fields. The real Sally was more than welcome to stay, but her pseudo-truckdriver alter ego had to go. When Burt finished speaking, Sally just stood there mortified and silent. Then she broke down and started crying in front of the whole crew. After that, she never uttered another obscenity in Burt's presence again.

Strangely enough, that first confrontation didn't put a damper on their budding romance. It actually brought them closer together, because Sally was almost thankful for being chewed out. She felt she had so much to learn—she felt so inadequate in so many ways. No wonder she viewed Burt's criticism as a loving gesture, not harsh reproof. It would be the pattern of things to come: All through their relationship, Sally's primary motivation would be to please Burt. If he thought she was making a fool of herself, then she had to stop it, switch gears, do whatever was necessary to change. That was that—she had no other choice.

But it wasn't a totally one-sided relationship—on occasion, Sally knew how to wield power, too. If Burt seemed the stronger of the two personalities, he was also the more reckless, and Sally gradually became a tempering force in his life. In a sense, they supported each other. On one level, he molded her; on another level, she managed him.

When it came to Burt's health, Sally had no qualms about taking control. It was quickly apparent to her that he was trying to burn the candle at both ends, and things came to a head soon enough. Shortly after they began shooting *Smokey and the Bandit*, Burt's hypoglycemia (low blood sugar) got so out of hand that at times he could barely leave his dressing room. That's when Sally stepped in and became his self-appointed nurse and bodyguard.

Burt had been suffering from dangerously low blood sugar for more than a year, but at first doctors had pooh-poohed his condition. They blamed his recurring malaise on stress. Even though he had all the symptoms of hypoglycemia—fainting, vomiting, fatigue, rapid heartbeat, and occasional difficulty breathing—a four-hour glucose test had failed to pinpoint the disease. (Later, he underwent a more strenuous six-hour glucose test which finally revealed the problem.) Meanwhile, during that year of progressive deterioration—and misdiagnosis—Burt had continued to drink and take Valium, both of which only aggravated the condition.

On-screen and in public, Burt managed to look as strong and handsome as ever, but there was no way that he could hide his illness from close friends, especially Sally. She realized that he was emotionally as well as physically drained, and fear, more than anything, was taking a heavy toll. For an entire year he'd suffered from a variety of debilitating symptoms and yet doctors couldn't explain what was really wrong with him. The stress of not knowing had probably been as damaging, in its own way, as his drinking or poor diet.

Once Burt was properly diagnosed, Sally set out to help him rectify things. When the doctors put him on a two-hour feeding schedule, to raise his blood sugar level and maintain it, Sally became a watchdog. She hovered over Burt day and night, making sure that he never skipped a mini-meal or ate the wrong thing.

She also encouraged him to cut himself off from false friends and hangers-on who were draining him emotionally. According to Sally, there were people surrounding him who were "just eating him up . . . He didn't have the ability to say, 'No, go away from me.'" They were leeches who called themselves friends—glorified gofers and good ole boys— who wandered on and off the set freely. Because of their influence, Burt's life was a constant circus. True, he condoned, even actively encouraged, their presence, but now all that had to change. Sally believed he'd never get well with so many demands on his time and energy. As her relationship with Burt intensified, many of the hangers-on began to fade into the background.

Without question, right from the start Sally and Burt both derived something vital from the relationship. He gave her confidence and a sense of her own highly potent femininity; she gave him structure and stability in his life. They were good for each other, because the symbiosis was truly mutual.

Sally immediately earned high points from Burt's best friend, Hal Needham, who was directing *Smokey and the Bandit*. (Needham had been living in the guest house on Burt's Bel-Air estate since 1972, when Needham's marriage had broken up.) It was originally Needham's idea to team Burt with the former Flying Nun, and her work on the film didn't disappoint him. Her TV training stood her in good stead. She was a quick study, punctual, and flexible when it came to changing her acting approach to a scene. In Needham's words, "She was certainly no prima donna." But what really endeared her to the cast and crew—and made her romance with Burt escalate, Needham believed—was Sally's attentiveness during Burt's siege of hypoglycemia. She had seen him at his worst and she wasn't intimidated by it. Her concern for the guy was genuine. She wasn't in love with the sex symbol—she cared deeply for the man himself. Perhaps for the first time in a relationship, Burt could let down his guard and drop the macho-man pose. He didn't have to play the tough wisecracker off-screen as well as on. With Sally it was okay to let a few warts show.

The film itself proved to a be a lucky turning point for them both. It did phenomenally well at the box office, outgrossing every other movie that year except *Star Wars*. It was a bigger hit than Woody Allen's *Annie Hall*, Steven Spielberg's *Close Encounters of the Third Kind*, and Neil Simon's *The Goodbye Girl*.

What made *Smokey* the must-see comedy of 1977? Three factors apparently combined to make the difference. First of all, luck. The CB-radio craze had just taken hold, and the country was definitely ready for a film that glorified the phenomenon. Secondly, chemistry. Burt and Sally's screen relationship was magical and refreshing. And thirdly, a great patchwork job. The actors really worked hard to make a silk purse out of a script that, by everyone's admission, had started out as a sow's ear. Burt later confided to *Playboy's* Lawrence Linderman that Jackie Gleason, who played the villain, "pretty much ad-libbed his entire part, Sally Field . . . is a terrific improviser, and I'm real good at it, too."

After the completion of *Smokey and the Bandit,* Sally felt she needed a change of pace, so she agreed to team with "Happy Days" star Henry Winkler in *Heroes,* the story of a frenetic Vietnam veteran involved in a crazy, cross-country chase after wealth and success. Sally played the girl he fell in love with along the way. The film wasn't very successful at the box office, but was notable for one other casting choice: Harrison Ford, at that time still an unknown, made a featured appearance in it.

Winkler had specifically requested Sally as his co-star because of her work in *Sybil.* He considered her performance in that four-hour movie "the most dynamic achievement ever on TV." And like Burt Reynolds, he also felt a professional bond with Sally on the basis of a shared image problem. Winkler was pretty much trying to do the same thing she was—make the transition from television to film—and he was hoping that *Heroes* would help him do that. He desperately wanted the public to accept him as someone other than Fonzie, the tough-talking, motorcycle-riding semi-delinquent he played with such greasy aplomb on "Happy Days." But Winkler was not destined to be as successful in shedding his TV image as Sally was. He never made a blockbuster movie and wound up staying on "Happy Days" for ten years—till the bitter end in 1974. After that, he did a slow fadeout of the acting arena and became much more successful as a TV producer, packaging and developing situation comedies.

Perhaps—as far as Henry Winkler's future went—the writing was already on the wall when they began filming *Heroes.* On location at an auto-racing track in Petaluma, California, director Jeremy Kagan had to stop the cameras over and over again as hordes of fans, who had to be restrained behind police barricades, kept interrupting filming with their shrieks of "Hey, Fonz!" That day Winkler drew ten times the number of cheers from the crowds than Sally did, but maybe that was all for the best. It only raised his typecasting quotient higher, while it obviously meant that America was beginning to forget about Sally's high-flying days on the situation-comedy treadmill.

But Sally's road to motion-picture stardom wasn't paved with gold—not yet. Perhaps if *Heroes* had done better at the box office, Sally might have been able to feel a little more adventurous in choosing her next project, but she didn't seem to be threatening Fonda or Keaton yet. Moreover, she still felt shaky on her own, so she did the only safe thing: She ran right back to Burt's side and co-starred with him in two more films in quick succession. It looked like Burt and Sally had the comedy market all sewed up—and if their style of humor wasn't nearly as sophisticated as Hepburn and Tracy's had once been, well, they were a lot cuter than Cheech and Chong—and a lot less neurotic than Woody Allen and his leading ladies!

Sally's first successful rematch with Burt was in *The End,* a prickly black comedy about a man with a terminal illness who contemplates suicide. (Reynolds also made his directorial debut with this film.) Despite the semi-serious theme, making that movie was one of the happiest times in Burt and Sally's sojourn together. It became a real family affair. Burt generously gave cameo roles to Sally's mother, stepfather, and sister. He particularly enjoyed working with Jock Mahoney, whose outlook and temperament were pretty much cut from the same piece of cloth as Burt's. They were macho brothers under the skin. In fact, on the home front, Jock had become Burt's biggest booster. In 1977 he told *The Star*, "Burt is beautiful people. He is a real gentleman. We have a tremendous amount in common. We're both Aquarians, both actors and former stuntmen." Then he added enthusiastically, "If Burt and Sally do decide to get married, I'd be thrilled."

The End represented an interesting departure for Burt. With its heavy emphasis on death, it was hardly upbeat or escapist. The script, written by Jerry Belson, had originally been intended for Woody Allen, who had passed on it. After that, the project hung around Hollywood for years, shuffled from one studio desk to the next. No major star would touch it because of the downbeat subject matter. When Burt got wind of the script, however, he jumped at the chance to do it (perhaps because of his own life-threatening bout with hypoglycemia). Moreover, Burt was in a position to follow through, which some other potential script rescuers weren't. He was one of the few stars with enough clout to bully a major studio (United Artists) into actually mounting the production. Interestingly enough, though, Burt and Sally's presence—despite their huge success with *Smokey and the Bandit*—wasn't considered a solid enough bet at the box office. To help entice audiences to see the picture, a stellar supporting cast was added: Joanne Woodward, Kristy McNichol, Robby Benson, Norman Fell, Myrna Loy, David Steinberg, and Carl Reiner.

Sally liked the fact that her role would be far more demanding than her mainly slapstick appearance in *Smokey* had been. This time she'd be playing a character who cried, whined, and stamped her feet in the middle of thoroughly unappealing temper tantrums. In fact, as Burt envisioned it, Sally's role would be the shocking, unsavory flip side of Gidget. "In this film I may look like the shiny, all-American cheerleader again, but I'm not," said Sally. "For starters I live in the filthiest, most disgusting house you've ever seen in your life."

The End was certainly off the beaten track, but despite its dark tapestry, it did reasonably well financially. While nowhere near as successful as most other Reynolds flicks, it eventually earned $20 million and did nothing to diminish his stature as a box-office kingpin.

That same year—1978—Sally and Burt also made *Hooper,* a definite return to the kind of throwaway, feel-good movies that were Burt's real trademark. In this loony, light-hearted effort, once again directed by Hal Needham, Sally played the girlfriend of an aging Hollywood stuntman (Reynolds), and the script was little more than an out-and-out valentine to the guys who really take the punches in all those macho movies (a kind of forerunner of TV's "The Fall Guy," if you will). It was a film in which male characters predominated—with their on- and off-set stunts, brawls and chases—but Sally had no qualms about accepting a decidedly supporting role. "I did it because I wanted to be close to Burt," she admitted.

While she was down in Tuscaloosa, Alabama, filming *Hooper,* Sally got an urgent call from her agent back in Los Angeles. He relayed the news that Martin Ritt wanted to meet with her. Ritt was the man who'd directed classy Academy Award contenders like *Hud, Sounder,* and *The Spy Who Came in From the Cold.* Now he was getting ready to make a film called *Norma Rae,* about a poor Southern factory girl who becomes a rabid union organizer. He'd already seen more than a dozen actresses, but—and it was an awfully slim "but," her agent cautioned her—Ritt was willing to consider Sally for the coveted title part.

She made arrangements to fly back to L.A. as soon as possible. At that time, she was earning $150,000 a picture—a meager sum in movie-star terms—while Burt's salary was in the $2-million range. *Norma Rae* might not put her on a financial par with her mentor/screen partner/boyfriend, but in other ways it would radically tip the scales in Sally's favor. Their relationship would never be the same again.

7. It's Not How You Play The Role That Counts . . . It's Whether You Win or Lose!

In 1949 Jane Wyman won an Academy Award for her portrayal of a deaf girl in *Johnny Belinda*. Jane's performance was nothing short of brilliant, to be sure, but is that what really clinched her victory? No, not quite. The truth is there were other factors at work. For starters, Jane had recently given equally stunning performances in *The Lost Weekend* and *The Yearling*, and on both occasions the Motion Picture Academy had chosen to overlook her work. So there was definitely an element of better-late-than-never in her *Johnny Belinda* win.

Wyman had also put her personal life on the line—and it's no secret that Oscar can be unabashedly sentimental at times. While making *Johnny Belinda*, Wyman had suffered a miscarriage and her marriage to Ronald Reagan had fallen apart. Talk about valor on the set above and beyond the call of duty.

But those factors alone—compelling as they were—might not have propelled her to victory. According to Hollywood insiders, what really made everyone vote for her—instead of voting for Olivia de Havilland or Barbara Stanwyck, the two other favorites that year—was the fact that Jane had achieved her *Johnny Belinda* success by the skin of her teeth. That's what Oscar really loves: an underdog who succeeds against all odds. It was common knowledge that Warner Brothers had originally tried to bury the film instead of releasing it because Jack Warner—the studio boss who wasn't exactly Jane Wyman's dearest friend—foolishly thought he had a clinker on his hands. He was convinced that audiences would flee the theater in droves, repelled by the story of a deaf girl who endures one horror after another (including rape) and never utters a word on-screen. Jack Warner was dead wrong, of course. Audiences flocked to see the film, and Jane Wyman had the last laugh. Giving her the Oscar, then, was Hollywood's way of acknowledging her hard-earned triumph.

Over the years that same theme—David outwitting Goliath—has been a recurring Oscar-night motif. The harder an actress has to fight to get a role, the better her chances of capturing that thirteen-and-a-half-inch gold statuette. Anna Magnani was the producers' first choice to play the lead in *Two Women;* she dropped out of the project, so Sophia Loren won an Oscar for doing it. Warner Brothers wouldn't let Julie Andrews re-create her Broadway role in *My Fair Lady* because the studio felt she lacked box-office charisma. Audrey Hepburn got the part, but Julie got an Academy Award for *Mary Poppins.*

When feisty little stars outfox big studios, they invariably win the race because Academy voters love the thrill and excitement of a real upset. There's nothing quite like seeing a dark horse suddenly break out of the pack and win by a nose! In a sense, Sally Field was one of the most renegade fillies Hollywood had ever seen—and that goes a long way toward explaining her astonishing Academy Award triumph in the 1979 Best Actress race.

What really made her win that year—and win so big? Was she being honored strictly on the basis of her breathtaking performance alone, or were other considerations involved? Let's face it, the turnaround was nothing short of miraculous. After denying her talent for so many years, here was Hollywood and the entire motion-picture establishment suddenly falling all over themselves to shower her with every conceivable acting award—the Golden Globe, lots of high-toned critics' trophies, and ultimately the Oscar itself. Well, maybe her behind-the-scenes struggle impressed them as much as her on-screen battles did. They knew that Sally Field wasn't Martin Ritt's first choice to play Norma Rae. Hell, she wasn't even his third or fourth.

20th Century-Fox had campaigned hard for a star with guaranteed box-office appeal. They were particularly enamored of Jane Fonda, who was riding high as a result of *Julia, California Suite,* and *Coming Home.* But when Martin Ritt asked her to play Norma Rae, she turned him down cold. Fonda felt the part wouldn't be a challenge for her, because she really was a social activist like Norma Rae, maybe a little more educated and polished, but just as ornery and outspoken. She preferred creating women on-screen who diverged from her real-life persona, not women who mirrored it.

After Fonda's turndown, Ritt approached several other bankable stars, but didn't have any more luck. In quick succession, Jill Clayburgh, Marsha Mason, and Diane Keaton all declined the opportunity to play Norma Rae, either because of prior commitments or because they felt the role just wasn't right for them. So Sally became the main contender almost by default.

(Ironically, Sally—who was mentioned for the part almost as an afterthought—eventually had the last laugh. In the 1979 Oscar race she defeated Jill Clayburgh, Marsha Mason, and Jane Fonda, nominated for *Starting Over, Chapter Two,* and *The China Syndrome* respectively. The fifth nominee was Bette Midler, for *The Rose.*)

It was Martin Ritt's secretary, Golda, who played behind-the-scenes angel. She brought up Sally's name after he had completely exhausted his A-list of potential Norma Raes. Like *Stay Hungry* director Bob Rafelson, Ritt's first reaction was, "Sally who?" But his secretary managed to persuade him to sit through a screening of *Sybil.* On the basis of that, he was willing to give Sally an interview.

So Sally put *Hooper* on hold and flew up from Tuscaloosa. Her first meeting with Ritt went even better than she'd expected. Artistically, the rapport was immediate.

Ritt told her that he wanted an actress who could submerge herself in the part and not come up for air.

Sally assured him she was exactly that kind of actress—and there was something so determined and compelling in her attitude that Ritt actually believed her. He later said, "There wasn't a better actress for that part in the world. Sally is indomitable."

It was the start of a beautiful relationship—part mentor and student, part father and daughter.

But even though Ritt now had his Norma Rae, the film was a long way from being made. The studio had to fall in love with Sally Field, too.

So Ritt next set about winning over 20th Century-Fox, whose executives weren't so easy to convince. To date Sally's only successful films were *Smokey and the Bandit* and *The*

End—and the fact was that Burt Reynolds had dominated them both. Without his presence—in a film like *Heroes,* for instance—Sally had flopped. But Ritt stuck to his guns and finally managed to persuade the studio that the problem with *Heroes* was the material, not the actress. After an interminable round of meetings, conferences calls, hedging, hemming, hawing, and more meetings, they agreed to take a chance on her. Besides, Sally's bargain price—a mere $150,000—was an obvious selling point, too.

After Sally came on board, Ritt began to fill in the rest of the blank spaces. Beau Bridges was cast as Norma Rae's husband, and Ron Liebman was hired to play Reuben Marshasky, the Jewish union organizer from New York who goads Norma Rae into fighting the powerful mill owners. Pat Hingle and Barbara Baxley took on supporting roles.

From the start, Sally put herself totally in the director's hands. Martin Ritt became her mentor—a beloved authority figure—much like her former acting coach, Lee Strasberg, had once been. Ritt encouraged Sally to take risks onscreen—to try things that another actress might have balked at—and she willingly obliged. In *Norma Rae,* for the first time in her career, she wore jeans (not the designer kind), cheap T-shirts, and the least makeup possible. She sweated visibly on screen; she cursed; she even suffered a nosebleed. And she gave one of the grittiest—and most moving—performances in movie memory.

At the start of the film, Norma Rae's lover told her, "You got dirt under your fingernails and you pick your teeth with a matchbook." It was a perfect description. With that single line of dialogue, the Flying Nun finally disintegrated before our eyes—and a brand-new Sally Field was born.

On March 11, 1979—not long after the film opened—Vincent Canby, the esteemed film critic of *The New York*

Times, described Sally as "a small woman with a waist tinier than Scarlett O'Hara's and with a large talent controlled by intelligence." He considered her work in *Norma Rae* a triumph of the first magnitude. Canby wrote that "the performance she gives here is as big as the screen that presents it."

Critics all around the country were quick to echo his sentiments, and Sally Field became the new darling of the art-film set. All through the year she racked up one victory after another. She won the Cannes Film Festival award, the New York Film Critics award, the Los Angeles Film Critics award, the National Board of Review award, the National Society of Film Critics award, and the Golden Globe for Best Dramatic Actress. In fact, the only major race she lost that year was the British Academy Award: Jane Fonda picked up that trophy for *The China Syndrome.*

Along the way, there were also a few lessons in humility, too. An interesting thing happened at the Cannes Film Festival. When *Norma Rae* was screened for the assembled VIPs, there was stunned silence at the end of the film. Then the audience in the Grand Baroque Theater stood up and applauded, yelling "Bravo! Bravo!" while Sally—the center of all that spontaneous attention—just sat there and cried. A week later the film festival's jury awarded her the Best Actress prize. But, in Europe at least, it was still a case of "Sally who?" Despite all the acclaim, Sally had not been elevated into Jane Fonda's or Glenda Jackson's league, and she was about to have a rude awakening, indeed.

The night of the awards ceremony she was practically left out in the cold. The woman in charge of seating didn't recognize Sally and refused to let her into the auditorium. Sally just stood outside the stage door getting pushed and shoved by the unruly crowds, while the *paparazzi* completely ignored her, too. It was a totally humiliating moment—even the Flying Nun never had nights like this! Luckily, when Jack Lemmon (the festival's Best Actor winner) arrived, he happened to notice poor Sally standing around like a lost sheep. He plucked her out of the crowd, took her arm, and led her back to the stage door where she'd already been turned away. "Don't worry, she's with me," he gallantly announced as he quickly stepped inside with the evening's most acclaimed (but most forgotten) actress.

Of course, when the Oscar nominations came out in February 1980, Sally's name led the list of Best Actress contenders. Irving Ravetch and Harriet Frank Jr. were also nominated for their *Norma Rae* screenplay, along with songwriters David Shire and Norman Gimbel for the film's haunting theme song, "It Goes Like It Goes." The film itself was in the running for Best Picture, but there was one serious omission: Martin Ritt's name was missing from the list of that year's Best Director candidates. The Motion Picture Academy had completely overlooked him.

It was not the first time Ritt had gotten the shaft. The same thing had happened in 1972 when Ritt's film *Sounder* was nominated for Best Picture, along with Paul Winfield and Cicely Tyson for Best Actor and Actress, and his name was omitted in the directors' race. Indeed, despite the fact that Martin Ritt has long been considered one of Hollywood's pre-eminent directors, he has only been nominated once—for the 1963 Paul Newman/Patricia Neal film, *Hud*.

It's true that Alfred Hitchcock, Ingmar Bergman, Steven Spielberg, Richard Brooks, and Sidney Lumet—to name just a few giants—have never won directing Oscars; nevertheless, none of them would have turned the trophy down. Martin Ritt was so put out that Sally had to cajole him into attending the Academy Award ceremonies. She told Hollywood columnist Marilyn Beck, "He was very hurt that he didn't receive a nomination for the film. And I don't blame him."

It was a year of strange parallels in the Oscar derby. Meryl Streep—the leading Supporting Actress contender for her portrayal of an absentee mother in *Kramer vs. Kramer*—came to her role by a fluke much as Sally Field had done. Kate Jackson, who was director Robert Benton's first choice for the part, had had to bow out because of a schedule conflict with her TV series, "Charlie's Angels." Even more significantly, a situation very similar to the Martin Ritt nomination snub developed with Burt Reynolds's film *Starting Over*. Although his two leading ladies, Jill Clayburgh and Candice Bergen, were nominated as Best Actress and Best Supporting Actress respectively, Burt himself was ignored by Academy voters. Hollywood was still refusing to accept him as a serious actor, despite the fact that his reviews for the film were consistently impressive.

So Sally found herself entering the Oscar arena with mixed feelings—thrilled at her own success, but angry and disappointed over the shabby treatment the two most important men in her life had received. Still and all, she was determined to run a good race. It would have been out of character for her to do anything else.

At that point, Sally didn't have much clout in the movie industry. It was the first year she could even vote in the Oscar race. (Her two sponsors for membership in the Academy of Motion Picture Arts and Sciences were Burt Reynolds and Carol Burnett.) There was a part of her that truly dreaded going to the awards—she hated all the hype and hoopla, the whole circus atmosphere of Oscar night. But if she were a no-show, some people might think she was thumbing her nose at the whole thing. Besides, attending the award ceremonies might have one added benefit: In case she won, she wanted the chance to thank Martin Ritt publicly for casting her as Norma Rae and for guiding her to success. She felt she owed him that much, especially in light of the fact that he had been denied a nomination.

She was nervous about confronting her fellow nominees, but the evening turned out far differently than she'd imagined. Just before the telecast, Sally found herself sitting in a semicircle with Jane Fonda, Jill Clayburgh, Bette Midler, and Meryl Streep—and suddenly they felt more like sorority sisters than opponents. "It was us against the TV cameras. It was just like being at the prom," Sally said. "We were all wishing each other luck and telling one another that our hair and makeup looked fine. There was no feeling of competitiveness at all."

When all was said and done, when all the ballots had been counted and all the envelopes duly torn and crumpled—*Kramer vs. Kramer* was the big winner of the evening. It walked off with Best Picture honors plus statuettes for Dustin Hoffman and Meryl Streep, and two Oscars for Robert Benton as director and screenwriter. Melvyn Douglas (*Being There*) was chosen Best Supporting Actor, but *Norma Rae* wasn't completely overlooked. Aside from Sally Field's citation as Best Actress, "It Goes Like It Goes" was named best song of the year.

Sally's win was nothing short of spectacular. It was the first time an actress known mainly as a television performer had managed to capture an Academy Award for a leading role. (In 1969 "Laugh-In" graduate Goldie Hawn had won a Supporting Actress trophy for *Cactus Flower*.) Generally, the reverse happened. After their film careers started to decline, Oscar-winning stars like Jane Wyman, Shirley Booth, and Donna Reed all condescended to do TV series. In the wake of Sally's triumph, the cinema world's bias against television celebrities changed somewhat; in fact, in the 1980s television suddenly emerged as a major supplier of motion-picture talent. Tom Hanks, Shelley Long, Mary Tyler Moore, Eddie Murphy, and most of the "Saturday Night Live" gang all made the transition from television to film, although (except for Moore) the thrust was mainly comedy.

Sally's reaction to her Oscar win was pure amazement. For weeks beforehand, she had gone around informing everyone that she was sure she'd lose—and her first impulse after winning was to laugh the whole thing off. She announced that the Motion Picture Academy had definitely gone down a notch or two in the class department by trying to elevate her to the same level occupied by legends like Katharine Hepburn and Bette Davis. She self-deprecatingly compared her victory to the Groucho Marx quip, "I wouldn't want to be in a club that would have me as a member."

But that was just plain dumb insecurity rearing its head. Underneath it all, Sally was ecstatic and she took her victory very seriously. Her triumph in *Norma Rae* represented the culmination of a twelve-year struggle to gain respect in Hollywood. She had finally shaken off her ponytail-and-purity image.

There was only storm cloud on the horizon—a minor one at that, but one that refused to evaporate. Crystal Lee Sutton, the millworker from Burlington, North Carolina, whose real-life story had provided much of the basis for the script of *Norma Rae,* became a loud and unhappy counterpoint to the film's success story. Her gripe was that she didn't get a fair shake from 20th Century-Fox.

According to newspaper accounts published in 1985, Sutton had "fallen on hard times" and was petitioning Sally

Field for help. She'd been laid off from her factory job (where she was still earning $3.35 an hour) and all her attempts to capitalize on the success of *Norma Rae* had failed. The film's producers had grossed over $12 million, but she certainly wasn't living off any of the profits. She had received only $52,000 (almost half of which was eaten up by taxes) in an out-of-court settlement when she had threatened to sue the studio for exploiting her story. Moreover, 20th Century-Fox had refused to even let her use a 16mm print of *Norma Rae* as part of a program she was trying to develop on the lecture circuit. But Crystal Lee didn't have much luck on the lecture circuit, anyway. A letter campaign to 250 different organizations had resulted in bookings for only three speaking engagements.

But Sally Field wasn't totally moved by Crystal Lee Sutton's plight. Sally felt that her mentor, Martin Ritt, was being unjustly painted in a bad light—and she was quick to jump to his defense. Sally publicly disputed the contention that *Norma Rae* was entirely Crystal Lee Sutton's story. According to Sally, the character was based on the experiences of five different women. Sally told the *Los Angeles Herald Examiner* that "the press has the impression that Marty and 20th Century-Fox exploited her [Crystal Lee Sutton] terribly, that she was never offered any money for the film. The fact is that Marty offered her $50,000, which her attorneys talked her out of taking . . ." (Later, she did take approximately that sum.)

At any rate, if things didn't turn out spectacularly for Crystal Lee Sutton, Sally Field wasn't entirely out of the woods yet herself. Despite the fact that *Norma Rae* brought her respect in filmdom with a capital R, her movie career was destined to sputter and stall a few more times yet. Unlike Meryl Streep or Sissy Spacek, she wouldn't move blithely from one serious-film triumph to the next just because she owned an Academy Award. A debacle called *Beyond the Poseidon Adventure* still lay ahead of her—and that would nearly sink her career.

Her romance with Burt Reynolds would soon be in trouble, too. In fact, winning the Oscar may have been the first step toward losing Burt.

8. "Lizzie and Starbuck"— Lovers, Partners, and Rivals

In Hollywood—a town where celebrities change partners as frequently as they change agents or hairdressers—few could hve predicted the intensity of he relationship that developed between Sally Field and Burt Reynolds. For a time, they seemed an almost indestructible twosome.

Burt—the centerfold turned superstar—and Sally—the bubblehead turned brilliant actress—were certainly an odd couple. Maybe the only thing they truly had in common was their mutual struggle to live down their pasts and put centerfolds and sitcoms behind them. They both wanted to be taken seriously. But Hollywood is a place where it's hard to change labels. And in the end maybe that's what did their relationship in.

Financially, Burt was one of the most successful cinema idols around; he was right up there with Clint Eastwood, Robert Redford, and Paul Newman. By 1979 he was the number-one box-office star in the country, and he hadn't missed a year in the top-ten list since 1973. But ultimately Sally got the jump on him. Artistically, she moved ahead, gaining attention for herself in one serious project after another, and far outdistanced him in the film world. To this day, Burt remains stereotyped as the king of lightweight comedies and car chases, except for an occasional detour into violent detective films. In a nutshell: Sally made the breakthrough into high-quality, three-dimensional roles, and Burt didn't. He's still waiting for his *Norma Rae*.

There's an old joke that Oscar has broken up more Hollywood couples than sex or money. Despite the obvious exaggeration, there's a definite ring of truth to it. Notice how Elizabeth Taylor's marriage to Richard Burton visibly began to deteriorate after she won an Academy Award for *Who's Afraid of Virginia Woolf?* and he didn't. Or take the case of British actress Maggie Smith, who gained an Oscar—and lost a husband (actor Robert Stephens)—after making *The Prime of Miss Jean Brodie* in 1969. The year before exactly the same fate had awaited Barbra Streisand, who snared a Best Actress trophy for her very first film, *Funny Girl*. Her husband, Elliott Gould, who was having a tough time making the transition from stage to film, walked out of the marriage soon afterward.

If Burt Reynolds and Sally Field had been married at the time she won her Oscar, they might have named *Norma Rae* co-respondent in their divorce action. But that's not the whole story. Even if Sally had been content just to remain Burt's trusting little shadow on-screen and off, and not advance her career separately from his, chances are they would have wound up in the same boat—sinking. Ego clashes were only the tip of the iceberg. Burt was flamboyant; Sally was not. He was Hollywood and she was a San Fernando Valley suburbanite right down to the core of her being. Sally had shopping malls in her bones, you might say; Burt had parties and penthouses.

They spent a lot of time trying to figure out their relationship—and exactly where they were headed—but never really got a joint itinerary worked out. In the late 1970s, for better or for worse, they remained a *couple,* whatever that meant. They were never quite engaged, never quite broken up—and even though they actually split for a time in the spring of 1980 (right before the Oscar telecast), the final break didn't come until more than a year after that.

Sally was certainly a different breed from most of the glamorous women who'd previously occupied center stage in Burt's life. She was hardly a free spirit like his ex-wife Judy Carne or a middle-aged powerhouse like Dinah Shore. According to some observers, Sally represented a real change for Burt, and maybe that was a large part of her charm. In temperament and outlook, Sally was actually closest to Miko Mayama, the young Japanese actress who lived with Burt for more than two years in the late 1960s. Like Sally, Miko was basically a homebody who loved feathering a nest. Both Miko and Sally brought order and stability into Burt's highly charged, hyperactive life. They got him to give up the late-night party circuit (at least for a while) and curl up in front of the TV with a pillow and some popcorn.

Work played a dominant role in the blossoming of the Field/Reynolds romance, too. In some ways, Sally and Burt were simply a classic case of co-stars who fell in love. They certainly weren't the first movieland couple who'd stepped into that trap. From the start, the chemistry between them was electric. Is it any wonder they got a little carried away doing too much homework together? Like Burton and Taylor, Hepburn and Tracy—even Vivien Leigh and Laurence Olivier—Burt and Sally worked so well together that collaboration became an all-consuming part of their lives. To a large degree, their on-screen partnering stimulated, and later supported, their off-screen love story. The plain fact is Sally and Burt couldn't keep away from each other: They made four films together in barely four years.

Even away from the studio, they didn't really take their makeup off. Burt and Sally spent endless hours at his house or hers rehearsing scenes just for fun. They'd sit around acting out *Cat on a Hot Tin Roof, The Front Page,* or *Barefoot in the Park* together. That Sunday-afternoon playacting was more stimulating than a lot of the screen acting they were getting paid to do. Lucrative as they were, scripts like *Smokey and the Bandit* and *Hooper* just didn't pack enough of a dramatic wallop to satisfy either of them artistically.

So, after their first few film ventures together, the next step was only logical. They put a dollar sign in front of the playacting and dove into another arena—live theater. Burt Reynolds and Sally Field set out to prove to themselves—and the world—that they were more than just a couple of Technicolor hacks. And they did so very successfully.

But they were wise enough not to tempt fate. For their first stage engagement, they found a tiny theater in West Palm Beach, Florida, where they co-starred in *Bus Stop.* The local reviews were good, but nothing to make Hume Cronyn and Jessica Tandy turn in their Actors Equity cards. Still and all, it was a good stretch for them both. Burt got a chance to let his super-macho guard down for a while and play an innocent, slightly dumb cowboy who was heartbreakingly touching at times. Sally was cast as Cherry, the peroxide-blonde barroom singer who became the object of the cowboy's affections. Sally, who hadn't portrayed many blatantly sexy women before, thrived on the challenge of breathing new life into a role that Marilyn Monroe had made famous. Their success in *Bus Stop* made them even hungrier to try their hand at more theater. Moreover, Burt was becoming increasingly enthusiastic about stage work from a business, as well as an artistic, point of view. He and Sally toyed with the idea of trying to launch their own production on Broadway, but quickly decided against it for three reasons: (1) Neither of them was anxious to move to New York, (2) the costs of mounting a Broadway production were astronomical, and (3) except for musicals, very few Broadway shows had much chance of success.

Besides, Burt had a much better idea: Why not start his own theater company right here in Florida—his home base—where he already felt comfortable and where there was a definite need for it? The Palm Beach area was certainly the kind of upscale community that would rush to support legitimate theater, if it was worthwhile and entertaining. And Burt had another motivation, too: He wanted to give something back to the business because the business had been so good to him. He felt the Burt Reynolds Dinner Theater, as he envisioned it, could help give other actors a leg up on the ladder of success. It would provide young, unknown actors with a new arena where they could try their wings, a safe harbor away from New York, Chicago, and L.A., where they could work at their craft and learn and make mistakes and even fall on their faces occasionally while they went that inevitably tortuous route from novice to professional. It was, in that sense, a unique idea: a highly commercial theater—one that would feature primarily mainstream American playwrights, not Strindberg and Chekhov—yet at the same time function as an intensive repertory training ground, a boot camp for actors.

The end result of that dream was the Burt Reynolds Dinner Theater, which was erected in Jupiter, Florida, a suburb of Palm Beach. From the start, Burt functioned mainly as producer and director, while many of his longtime actor pals—like Charles Nelson Reilly and Dom DeLuise—became founding members of Burt's new repertory company. Some of them even taught classes in basic theater skills. Shortly before the release of *Norma Rae,* Sally starred in *Vanities,* one of the dinner theater's first productions.

But it wasn't a pleasant experience. At the time, Burt was in Boston, filming *Starting Over* with Jill Clayburgh and Candice Bergen, so he wasn't available to direct Sally's production himself. Instead he assigned the project to one of his old friends—a director whom Sally innstantly disliked. Their first set of rehearsals served only to confirm her opinion. She thought the man was incompetent, and didn't hesitate to tell him so. She firmly believed he was ruining the play—and told him that, too. Then she began to worry that if the production was really awful, it might permanently damage the Burt Reynolds Dinner Theater (which was still struggling to establish a reputation for itself)—and she passed *that* message on, too. The firebrand actress and the intransigent director were locked in an awesome power struggle, and unfortunately Burt wasn't there to intercede. He tried to do as much mediating as he could on the phone from Boston, but it was a bad situation that only got worse. The director may have been Burt's friend, but Sally was Burt's girl—and the star of the play. Ultimately, the director bowed out of the production and was replaced.

A much happier situation developed when Sally actually co-starred with Burt in a revival of *The Rainmaker* at the dinner theater. She played Lizzie, the fussy old-maid heroine, and he was Starbuck, the con-man/miracle-worker who brings her out of her lonely cocoon—the roles that Katharine Hepburn and Burt Lancaster had portrayed in the acclaimed 1956 movie. Reynolds also directed the production. It was a hat he felt increasingly comfortable wearing. In some ways he felt *more* comfortable directing than he did acting, because directing gave him a kind of control and freedom he never experienced in front of the camera. Burt looked for more and more projects to stage. On the heels of *The Rainmaker*, he directed himself and Carol Burnett in a dinner theater production of *Same Time, Next Year*. It also had no trouble drawing substantial audiences.

According to Sally, Burt was a natural when it came to directing. And the special satisfaction he derived from being in control was particularly important to his psyche. "I think Burt gets more joy from directing than he does from acting," she said. Why? The reason seemed obvious: When he worked behind the scenes, he didn't have to live up to other people's expectations of himself—as he was forever locked into doing on-screen.

One reporter made an interesting point when reviewing Burt and Sally's production of *The Rainmaker*. At the end of the play, Lizzie doesn't run off with Starbuck, dazzling though he may be. She chooses a safer, more predictable life with someone else. Was there a hint of a real-life parallel at work here? Devoted as they were, Burt and Sally didn't seem to be moving in the direction of marriage—or anywhere near it. Like Starbuck and Lizzie, Burt had definitely mesmerized his girl-next-door leading lady and gently guided her out of her homebody shell, but Sally apparently wasn't dazzled enough to demand marriage. Instead, they just seemed to be drifting along.

In some ways they were close; in other ways not. Neither was the kind who surrendered even an inch of independence very easily; and for all their exclusivity as a couple, barriers remained. Sally and her children still led a down-to-earth suburban life. Burt still made his share of raucous headlines sans his on-and-off-screen consort. As far as Sally was concerned, weekdays were for the kids, weekends for

Burt; and she regularly divided her time between her own moderate-priced house in Studio City (she'd sold the beach house; it was too far to commute to work) and Reynolds's magnificent Bel-Air retreat (next door to Barbra Streisand). They were never more than a half-hour drive apart; nevertheless, it was still a world of difference from living together and sharing the same toothpaste and towels. But neither of them seemed ready for that. (Occasionally, they did share a getaway condo near his parents' ranch in Florida.)

They had no qualms, however, about publicizing the ingenuousness of their relationship. Their matching Trans Ams (his was silver; the one he gave her was black) were the talk of the gossip columns, and—carrying cuteness to an even more saccharine extreme—Sally's license plate read: BR S GRL (an abbreviation, of course, for "Burt's Girl").

They dined together nearly every night (Sally did the cooking) and socialized on a fairly regular basis with Burt's close pals and their wives. The inner circle included David (and Judy) Steinberg, Dom (and Carol) DeLuise, and Norman (and Karen) Fell. What about Sally's friends and their husbands? Well, if the roster of social contacts seemed a little one-sided, that was possibly more Sally's fault than Burt's. By her own admission, she was a hard person to get to know and had acquired few longtime friends during the first thirty years of her life. On the other hand, Burt was the ultimate hail-fellow-well-met. Originally a top college athlete, he never really lost that knack for hearty locker-room bravado. He seemed to accumulate new buddies everywhere he went—from the loftiest studio execs to the guys who came to clean the swimming pool.

Sometimes he treated Sally like one of the boys, too, but that perhaps was a built-in hazard of getting involved with a college jock-turned-stuntman-turned-actor (shades of Jock

Mahoney). When the relationship was going well, Sally was ecstatic. When it wasn't, her mood darkened perceptibly. During one of the calms between the inevitable storms, she exclaimed to an interviewer from *Redbook* that she and Burt couldn't get over how well-matched they were on every level. "We keep thinking maybe this is reincarnation," Sally sighed. "Do you think we knew each other in the past?"

But the picture wasn't always as rosy as Sally tried to maintain. When they were geographically apart, furiously embroiled in separate projects, fears and tensions grew. When they came together again for a new movie or a new stage production, things improved—at least for a while. But after *Norma Rae* nothing was ever quite the same. From the time Sally got on that plane in Tuscaloosa—in the middle of filming *Hooper*—to head for Hollywood and fight for the part of Norma Rae, her relationship with Burt was in serious jeopardy. It wasn't so much that he envied her success— Burt, in fact, pushed her to do it. It's just that *Norma Rae* finally gave her the wings she needed to fly on her own— and maybe that meant she didn't need Burt. Or at least she didn't need his professional tutelage. Once she came to rely so heavily on Martin Ritt for career advice, Burt's position as her number-one mentor began to wane.

By the time the 1980 Oscar telecast rolled around, Burt and Sally had reached an enormous impasse. Burt didn't accompany her to the ceremonies at the Dorothy Chandler Pavilion, and she very pointedly didn't thank him in her acceptance speech. The fact that she had been nominated for *Norma Rae*, while he'd been ignored for *Starting Over*, obviously hurt. Sally later confided to *Ladies' Home Journal* that winning the Oscar helped undermine the relationship. "Burt really thinks I went out after that Oscar because he thinks the award is so important. I don't," she said. "To me the work is the important thing." But, possibly, there was no way of making Burt understand that. Or possibly Sally was protesting just a bit too much. For such a noncompetitive Oscar winner, she had certainly made herself highly visible at all the right publicity events during the Academy Award voting period. As far as landing an Oscar was concerned, she didn't exactly commend her fate entirely to the gods.

There was certainly poetic justice in all this. Ever since they'd met, Burt had kept prodding Sally to be more politic about her career—to meet the right people, attend the right functions, shake the right hands. Apparently, he'd been an excellent teacher, for shy, insecure Sally had ultimately learned how to navigate her way right to the winner's circle at the Dorothy Chandler Pavilion. It's a shame she couldn't save a place for Burt.

9. Disaster!

The 1970s had been a time of tremendous change and growth for Sally Field. As the decade came to a close, she could look back on it all and justifiably wonder if she was indeed the same person who'd giggled her way to stardom in an oversize nun's coronet a little more than a decade ago. No, she was hardly the same person at all—and certainly not the same actress.

Professionally, she'd accomplished much, but often at the cost of her personal relationships. A failed marriage attested to that; and now, six years after her divorce, she was still basically "a wife in search of a home." Sally wasn't the kind who slipped in and out of relationships easily—Coulter Adams and Burt Reynolds were the only two men who had occupied any real space in her life since she'd left Steve Craig. Now she clung to Burt, even though it was increasingly obvious to them both that the fire between them had long since dwindled down to embers.

In the midst of all this came another upheaval in her life: the debacle of *Beyond the Poseidon Adventure*. It was a film that Sally had agreed to make against her better judgment—

a film that Burt had actively encouraged her to undertake—and it turned out to be a decision she regretted immensely.

The original *Poseidon Adventure,* released in 1972, had been a bona fide box-office smash; in fact, it became a model for other big-name, big-budget disaster movies of the 1970s. The idea for the original was simple enough: A luxury liner capsizes in a tidal wave and all the passengers have to sink or swim. Unfortunately, when it came to the sequel in which Sally appeared, it was the actors who had to stand by and try to save their careers from drowning.

Sally was offered the role in *Poseidon II* right after she made *Norma Rae,* but before she had any real inkling of the tremendous impact that *Norma Rae* would have on her career. If she'd known that she was going to be inundated with accolades galore, she probably would have turned down *Poseidon II* and forced herself to wait until something better came along. But at that point the kind of roles she really ached for still seemed light-years away, and Sally wasn't brave enough to hold out for them.

So part of her reason for saying yes to director Irwin Allen was her recurring fear of never working again. Another strong consideration was money. Doing a purely commercial film that she really didn't care about was a way of permanently upping her asking price. The *Poseidon II* producers were willing to pay her $350,000—$200,000 more than she'd earned on *Norma Rae.* If she accepted their offer, she'd be moving into a new salary bracket. No matter what film she did after that—whether it was *Sophie's Choice* or something on the level of *The Texas Chainsaw Massacre*—the producers would still have to pay her $350,000 and not a penny less. In Hollywood, actors rarely work for less than they got on their last picture. And that's the point that Burt kept stressing: Better salaries are just as important as better roles—in fact, they can help an actor get better roles because, for some strange reason, producers believe that higher-priced actors are more valuable assets than lower-priced ones. Box-office economics is a crazy, Catch-22 situation, but to survive in Hollywood you have to play the game, and that's what *Beyond the Poseidon Adventure* would enable Sally to do.

Aside from the financial lure, *Poseidon II* had one other thing to recommend it—a super-glossy cast (apparently, Sally wasn't the only Hollywood star in need of quick cash). The impressive roster of players included Michael Caine, Telly Savalas, Shirley Knight, Peter Boyle, Jack Warden, Shirley Jones, and Karl Malden. How bad could it be?

But Sally had second thoughts right after she signed on the dotted line. She was lowering her standards, and she knew it. One of the first people Sally called was Martin Ritt, but she could hardly get her words out. She was so ashamed of her decision that the minute she got on the phone she dissolved in tears. She felt Ritt would be disappointed in her—or at least that's what she wanted to believe, because deep down she was so disappointed in herself. But actually he was very understanding. No, he didn't think she should worry that the film would be a step down for her. No, she certainly wasn't prostituting herself. There's nothing wrong with doing purely commercial work. "People have to survive," he told her soothingly. "You have to feed your children. Don't hate yourself for it."

But on the set her inward dissatisfaction soon translated into strident personality conflicts with the director. Sally had such a disastrous relationship with Irwin Allen that making the film turned into the worst experience of her career. No amount of money, she soon realized, was worth doing a job you truly hated. But by the time Sally came to that conclusion it was too late to back out.

She brooded constantly on the set. The more she thought about it, the more she wished Burt had encouraged her to say no, instead of pushing her to say yes. "I needed somebody to tell me, 'Sally, stick to your guns. Don't do it. Wait for the right role. Have confidence in yourself,' but that's not what I heard," she recalled. The truth was this: Burt was an astute businessman—and his advice made perfect financial sense. Sally, however, had trouble justifying things strictly on a dollars-and-cents basis.

Was she right to blame Burt, though? After all, Sally was hardly wet behind the ears. She was a thirty-three-year-old woman with a long professional career already behind her. Certainly, she should have been capable of making her own decisions—and of taking responsibility for them.

Sally's entire stint on *Beyond the Poseidon Adventure* was an unrelieved horror story. According to published reports, she fought with director Irwin Allen nearly every day of shooting. Finally, it got so bad that the crew was practically taking bets on the precise moment that the next explosion would erupt. Was Allen truly "inadequate," as Sally later claimed? Or was it the fact that his style of directing differed substantially from a Martin Ritt or a Hal Needham—or even a Burt Reynolds—men she'd felt instantly comfortable with and practically idolized? Allen didn't pretend to be a friend or a father figure, but he was hardly a fly-by-night moviemaker. His films may not have won standing ovations at the Cannes Film Festival, but they certainly helped keep the studios he worked for financially solvent. Indeed, Allen, who specialized in catastrophic disaster flicks with colossal casts and dazzling scenes of destruction, was responsible for 1975's *The Towering Inferno*. With $50 million in gross re-

ceipts at the box office, it was at that time the most successful disaster movie ever made.

But what irritated Sally was Allen's disorganized approach
to shooting. He'd rearrange scenes, change the action, and
throw out whole pages of dialogue without a moment's notice. On occasion, he'd be feeding the actors brand-new lines
when the cameras were just about to roll. To some observers, that kind of spontaneity may have been the height of
creativity. Sally considered it the height of craziness.

The worst blowup came when Sally was filming a difficult
scene on a boat, and Allen couldn't get the shots he wanted.
Sally later told *Playgirl's* Celeste Fremon that because Allen
lacked the expertise required to shoot a scene on a moving
boat, he had to make drastic last-minute changes. He
furiously started rewriting all the action and dialogue in a
frantic attempt to simplify the scene and make it shootable.
But Sally lost patience and balked at the delay. When Allen—standing on another boat—started shouting new dialogue to her through a megaphone, she completely lost her
cool. She absolutely refused to follow his instructions.

"Just do it!" Allen shrieked.

"I will not!" Sally yelled back. She shouted that she'd been
hired to play the script that she'd originally seen, not the
one he was writing on the spot. Then she coldly informed
him that if he wanted to make any more changes, she'd be
perfectly glad to oblige him—on her terms. He could feel
free to discuss all revisions with her before they began
shooting each scene, not when she was already standing in
the middle of a rocking boat and the cameramen were ready
to roll. Furthermore, Sally announced, she absolutely
wouldn't stand for him screaming at her across the water. If
they had anything to settle, she wanted to be spoken to pri-
vately, in a civilized fashion.

There was stunned silence among the assembled bystanders. But Sally had left her director/nemesis speechless and, since she happened to be right (a minor point perhaps, but worth noting anyway), she actually got her way. After that blowup, the director and his "difficult" leading lady maintained an uneasy truce till the film was finished. At the wrap party, neither was much in the mood for forgiving or forgetting. Allen had lost face in front of his cast and crew. Sally had probably lost face as an actress with a "quality" reputation. (She felt her performance was so dreadful that reviewers and audiences alike would laugh her off the screen.) Both of them saw only one ray of hope in the whole mess: At least they'd never have to work together again.

Sally was so dismayed after *Poseidon II* that she couldn't wait to rush back to Burt. He was, after all, her safe harbor. She knew he was about to start filming *Smokey and the Bandit II* with Kate Jackson as his co-star, but Sally was suddenly zealous about working with him again. She campaigned hard to get her old role back in the sequel and Burt finally relented. So Kate was out and Sally was in. After her prison sentence on *Poseidon II,* she was overjoyed at the prospect of working with Hal Needham, Dom DeLuise, and the whole Reynolds entourage again. Sally was back where she belonged—with friends who cared about her. Of course, there was one new addition to the cast—a pregnant elephant! Transporting her cross-country would be the main thrust of the plot. Well, it wasn't exactly Tennessee Williams, but what the heck—at least it would be fun.

Once again—as in so many Burt-and-Sally productions—making the film turned out to be a family affair. *Smokey II* was shot on location partially in Henderson, Nevada, right outside Las Vegas, and on the first day of shooting Sally's son Elijah actually got to make his acting debut in a bit part.

An interesting situation developed when Sally and Elijah disagreed over how he should play his crucial scene (which involved intercepting a phone call from the Bandit). Sally wanted Elijah to throw the phone in the air, as an added comic touch, but he felt it was too gimmicky. Finally, Hal Needham had to arbitrate the mother-son dispute by announcing he'd film the scene both ways and decide which version to keep later.

As always, Sally's strong sense of professionalism never faltered. At the end of the film, Burt Reynolds inserted his famous screen trademark—a montage of uproarious outtakes while the final credits rolled. There were hysterical clips of Reynolds, Jackie Gleason, and just about everyone else keeling over with laughter when they forgot their lines. Only Sally was standing up straight. That's because she never blew a scene.

At times—despite the occasional bursts of friction—Burt and Sally seemed to have it all. They were the ideal couple, riding the crest of a perfect wave that, quite possibly, would never end. At a celebrity roast for Burt in Atlanta, Sally took her turn at the podium and had a high old time relentlessly ribbing her main man. Totally deadpan, she told the crowd: "The truth is the man is a sex maniac. The hotel installed a take-a-number machine outside his room. I got number 88, but the line moves fast." When Burt's turn came to respond, he quipped that he and Sally did have a wonderful relationship—past tense. Then he paused dramatically and announced to the hushed crowd, "You were privileged tonight to see it end."

That night everyone knew Burt was only joking, but eventually his involvement with Sally did end. After their pre-Oscar breakup, Burt tried to patch things up and the reconciliation worked for a while. He actually wooed Sally back when he appeared on NBC's *Today* show and declared that he still loved Sally very, very much. She was shocked and surprised to hear him say that. Burt had never made a point of publicly revealing his feelings before. Now he was obviously trying to mend his fences. In that same TV interview, Burt disavowed any feelings of jealousy about Sally's recent Oscar victory. "I was actually totally overjoyed about her winning the award, regardless of what you read in the press," he said. In fact, Burt emphasized all the encouragement he'd given her in going after the role. According to Burt, his first remark to Sally after reading the original script of *Norma Rae* was, "May I have the envelope, please?" He'd told all his friends that *Norma Rae* was going to make Sally a star. What he'd felt right from the beginning, Burt maintained, was pride in her accomplishment, not jealousy.

Sally was extremely touched by Burt's on-air confession, and for a time it brought them closer together again. But belated valentines weren't enough. They were growing apart, and there was no turning back for either of them. They couldn't move the clock back to that shy, tentative moment in 1976 when Sally had first phoned Burt to tell him thanks, but no thanks, she wasn't interested in burning up the silver screen with him.

Disengaging wasn't an easy process. It took them more than a year after their first split to come to a mutual final parting. They'd break up, get back together for a while, then break up all over again. In mid-1980 Burt went to New York to film *Paternity* with Lauren Hutton. At one point Sally flew into town to visit him and they dined out at Le Cirque, a trendy Manhattan eatery. When Sally went to the ladies' room, Burt ordered dessert for her—a Grand Marnier soufflé. The next morning *The New York Daily News* (apparently having overheard Burt and Sally squabble at the table) noted that "by the time she returned [from the ladies' room] the dessert had fallen flat. As romance often does."

All through their relationship, Sally had to endure rumors of Burt's alleged interludes with other women. She knew all about his past involvements with Dinah Shore and Tammy Wynette, but as the years progressed, the whispers and innuendoes of new liaisons became harder to bear. The newspapers had a field day conjecturing about supposed involvements with Lesley-Anne Down, Lauren Hutton, and even Sophia Loren. The Burt/Sophia business was truly absurd. The closest they ever came to meeting were a few business converations on the phone, when Sophia's husband, Carlo Ponti, came up with an interesting proposition. He wanted to team Sophia and Burt in a remake of *The Rose Tattoo*. It never got beyond the talk stage.

At first, the press enjoyed concentrating on Burt and Sally's true-blue devotion to each other. When that became boring, the tabloids took a new tack: painting Burt as the most agile bed-hopper since Errol Flynn and Sally as the poor trusting fool who was always the last to know about his scandalous indiscretions. She tried not to let the sensational headlines upset her, and didn't even bother wasting her time refuting them. But occasionally she lashed out at the gutter standards of the popular press. Interviewed by *McCall's*, Sally said, "They [the tabloids] don't care what's the truth and who it hurts. Every time Burt makes a movie without me, there are stories about his secret romance with the leading lady. . . ."

The fabrications were particularly harmful to her children, who didn't know when to believe them or not. When they'd show their mother headlines that screamed BURT LEAVES SALLY FOR NEW LOVE! she'd try to tell them to disregard garbarge like that. Those headlines were blatant lies, she explained. But then the boys would point to another headline that said RUSSIA INVADES AFGHANISTAN and ask, "Mom, is that a lie, too?"

In 1981 Burt began filming *Sharkey's Machine* with beautiful newcomer Rachel Ward—not Sally—as his co-star. Instead she went off to make *Absence of Malice* with Paul Newman. Since Burt was on location in Atlanta, and she was shooting *Absence* in nearby Florida, Sally would fly to Atlanta every Friday nght to spend the weekend with him. But their reunions were no longer cozy and romantic. According to newspaper reports, Sally would return to her own set on Monday morning "in a difficult and demanding mood after those sixty-odd hours with Burt." It made people wonder if Sally and Burt were spending their weekends making war, not love.

Ironically, near the end of the relationship, Burt kept pressuring Sally to marry him and she kept turning him down. Part of Burt's marriage kick, undoubtably, was his desire to be a family man before it was too late—he was almost forty-five. All of Hollywood knew how desperate he was to have children, and Sally herself had occasionally remarked that she wouldn't mind having a little girl after raising two sons. But by 1980 Sally's film career was too high-powered for her to seriously consider tying herself down to pregnancy and motherhood for a third time.

In the mid-1970s Burt had actually tried to adopt a child, but had been turned down by every agency because of his bachelor lifestyle. Sally's boys had long considered him a "surrogate father," but Burt had second thoughts about the supposed benefits of an instant family. He once remarked that he had strong reservations about becoming a step-father—he didn't want the headaches of raising someone else's children. He felt he'd wind up being responsible for disciplining them, keeping them out of trouble, and sending them off to college only to have them turn around one day and say, "You're not my father!" He confided that, as far as he could tell, stepfatherhood was "dealing yourself in for a lot of pain."

Obviously, Burt had a mass of confused and conflicting feelings on the subject of parenthood. And obviously those feelings became another source of turmoil in his relationship with Sally. When the final breakup came, Sally actually ordered Burt not to keep in touch with her sons. She wanted no more contact between them. According to Burt Reynolds's biographer Marc Eliot, she passed on the message that "his influence was no longer wanted or needed."

The final parting in 1981 was far from amicable. To put it succinctly, Burt and Sally did not remain friends. According to Sally, the biggest problem was that Burt had resented her growing independence. He really wanted her to "make brownies and rub his feet" and function as a permanent accessory on his arm.

Was that a totally accurate portrait of what really happened? Hadn't Burt pushed her to get ahead in movies? Hadn't he actively encouraged her to meet studio executives, prestigious casting people and producers, anyone who could possibly be of help to her career? Was that all just a very showy smokescreen? Probably not. But even Burt Reynolds is human. Would it be so unforgivable if he wanted to be the man who guided her to the top? Maybe—and it's a big maybe—Burt was only anxious for Sally to succeed as long as she succeeded on his terms, by following his advice and by passively allowing him to play Pygmalion to her Galatea.

Whatever the real cause of the breakup, and it was probably an accumulation of many things, emotionally they'd run the gamut together. Without question, Burt and Sally had invested five very intense years in each other. In the end, slamming out the door was hardly easy, quick, or painless. Sally knew she had to move on, but the thought of starting over was scary, to say the least. "There's something very comfortable and reassuring about a relationship that isn't brand-new," she admitted. "It's nice to have someone who you know will love you even when you look your worst."

With Burt she'd had that, and more. Knowing him had changed her forever. She was bound to get hurt again—after all, who doesn't?—but she'd never be a shy little girl again. The woman and the actress were one.

10. Back Roads and Bad Turns

In 1980—right after finishing *Smokey and the Bandit II* and before embarking on *Absence of Malice*—Sally eagerly jumped at the opportunity to reteam with Martin Ritt. He was the one director she truly trusted with her career—indeed, if the situation had called for it, she probably would have trusted him with her life.

Sally was hardly the first film actress to favor a particular director. Katharine Hepburn had long been devoted to George Cukor, who guided her to success in *The Philadelphia Story* and *Pat and Mike*. Ingrid Bergman and Grace Kelly always seemed at their best in Alfred Hitchcock movies. In more recent years, Diane Keaton and Mia Farrow were both molded into comedic screen personalities by Woody Allen.

The right director can make an actress appear electrifying on camera; the wrong director can force her to give a performance that's dull and stilted. Sally Field was thoroughly aware of that, and in Martin Ritt she had every reason to believe she had found the Svengali who'd finally help her unlock her true screen potential. She considered him a genius.

The project that Ritt came to her with was a real departure from *Norma Rae.* This time he wanted her to star in *Back Roads,* an offbeat comedy-drama about a pair of itinerant low-lifes who meet on the road, become traveling companions, and slowly but surely fall in love. Tommy Lee Jones, the brooding young actor who was drawing critical acclaim as Sissy Spacek's husband in *Coal Miner's Daughter,* would play the part of the washed-up prize fighter who drifts into Sally's life and captures her heart.

The script seemed simple and straightforward enough. As far as Sally's part was concerned, she wouldn't have to worry about too many elegant costume changes—all she'd really have to be was loudmouthed and scruffy. Well, actually a little more than just plain loudmothed and scruffy. In fact, if the nuns at the Convent San Tanco could have seen her filming *Back Roads,* they would have been shocked: This time she was playing a prostitute.

How do you get into the psyche of a character like that? Sally had once read that Shirley MacLaine had actually walked the streets with French prostitutes while researching her role in *Irma la Douce,* and Jane Fonda had consulted with high-priced Los Angeles call girls to prepare for her Oscar-winning role in *Klute.* But Sally felt other approaches could be just as effective, especially since the film she was making didn't dwell on intimate glimpses into her character's occupation.

Amy Post—the hard-edged hooker she was about to play—certainly wasn't the kind of woman that Sally could relate to on a personal basis, yet she honestly believed that her Method training would see her through. After all, actresses regularly played Lady Macbeth without committing murder—and how many King Lears were really mad? The trick then was to find some common ground with the character, some honest thread of emotion that would bind the actress's own experience with the character's. Sally told Hollywood columnist Army Archard that, if you really thought about it, in some way everyone knows what it's like to be a prostitute. "I've felt that kind of degradation," she said. "And haven't we all sold ourselves at one time or another, no matter who or what we are?"

What was Sally referring to? It wasn't hard to figure out. Too many times in the past, she felt, she'd sold her talent for a few pieces of silver—grasped at projects that were unredeemably mediocre—simply in order to get work. Maybe playing Amy Post, a streetwalker on the run who's no longer really comfortable with her tawdry life, would have a cathartic effect. Maybe in the process of discovering what made Amy tick, Sally would finally get a chance to exorcise some of her own ghosts.

Like *Norma Rae, Back Roads* was set against a Southern backdrop. Shooting began in New Orleans, then moved on to Brownsville, Texas, and Mobile, Alabama. The cast was small and personally handpicked by Ritt. Aside from the two leads, it included Michael V. Gazzo, a former Oscar nominee for *Godfather II,* and a young actor named David Keith, who was destined to achieve stardom one year later for his portrayal of a tragic Air Force cadet in *An Officer and a Gentleman.* They all set out on location with high hopes for the project, but fate wasn't quite with them this time. Ritt and company got bogged down in problems almost at once.

From the start, the weather was uncooperative. In order to get the right cinematic "look," Ritt needed warm weather and sunshine, but when the cast and crew arrived in Brownsville, a record-breaking heat wave was in progress. At first, it seemed futile to move to another location. After all, how long could the scorching temperatures possibly last? As it turned out, a lot longer than anyone could have predicted. The sweltering heat persisted for days without any sign of relief, and even the local population deserted the streets for the safety of their air-conditioned homes and offices. After a while the weather became physically debilitating. Fatigue, nausea, and stomach cramps were common complaints on the set. It was hardly a promising situation. Production had practically ground to a halt, and if things continued at this rate, it looked like the cast might be marooned in Brownsville forever.

Realizing there was only one way out of this mess, Ritt made a crucial decision. He elected to shoot all the remaining scenes at night, when the weather would be substantially cooler.

Under the new schedule, working conditions were at least bearable, but still far from ideal, for night shooting brought its own set of agonies. Available light was a big problem. In order to shoot outdoors in the evening hours (when, obviously, there was no sunlight to light the set) a huge array of artificial lights had to be strung up all around the location site. Working with those lights was no picnic, and the actors fairly roasted under the added wattage.

There was another disadvantage, too. Night filming took a heavy toll on some people's health, especially on those actors and crew members who were poor sleepers to begin with. Once the company switched over to an after-dark shooting schedule, everyone had to completely rearrange their sleeping habits. Now they were staying up till all hours of the night filming, then sacking out during the day. Not everybody could adjust. Ironically, Ritt himself was unable to adapt and began suffering from insomnia. (In retrospect, considering the serious health problems he developed soon after filming was finished, *Back Roads* was probably made at an enormous cost to his own health.)

Sally went into the production determined to be a trouper. If Katharine Hepburn could survive living in the jungle while making *The African Queen,* a little prairie dust in her coffee wasn't going to defeat her. But even Sally's resiliency was put to the test: She proved particularly sensitive to the Texas heat. When the thermometer climbed to 115 degrees and refused to drop, she broke out in a nasty skin virus that covered her from chin to toe. She literally felt like she wanted to jump out of her skin. It made her irritable and short-tempered on the set, and there was an added worry—the cinematic effect. Sally certainly couldn't be seen covered with hives on-screen. So, to cover the blemishes, special body makeup had to be applied every day before she could face the camera. That took extra time and only made Sally even grumpier. The whole thing was a painful nuisance, and damned embarrassing. For the first time in her career, Sally had to turn down all interview and photo requests. She was too ashamed to be seen in public until her rash cleared up.

Thankfully, heat waves—and even skin conditions—don't last forever. Nobody was sorry to say goodbye to that location site.

After finishing up in Brownsville, the crew moved on to Mobile, Alabama—and that's where Sally found herself on Mother's Day 1980. Both her sons were back home in Los Angeles, but Eli sent her a very loving wish-we-were-with-you note that Sally taped up in a prominent place inside her dressing trailer. Burt Reynolds (with whom she'd recently reconciled) also sent greetings—a bouquet of flowers and hard candies with a bright yellow streamer that read HAPPY MOTHER'S DAY, SALLY.

Nevertheless, Sally was lonely. She was separated from all the people she loved, far from home, and bogged down in a difficult acting assignment. Filming seemed to be dragging on endlessly, and she was beginning to sense—with a sinking feeling in the pit of her stomach—that *Back Roads* wasn't exactly turning out to be a masterpiece. But it was only a vague feeling at this point, and she couldn't really allow herself to face that possibility. She had too much faith in Martin Ritt. His judgment couldn't possibly be wrong.

The physical discomforts of the rural Southern locations were compounded by the fact that Sally and her leading man didn't have a terrific relationship. Actually, that was putting it mildly. At times they were barely civil to each other. While rehearsing one scene, Jones had grabbed her by the arm and refused to let go. Sally lost her temper and sank her teeth right into his hand. Then Jones, who was really enraged now, ran after her and threatened to disfigure her face. Sally made no bones about her dislike for him. "He was a bad guy as far as I'm concerned," she later declared.

The only bright spot as far as Sally was concerned was the fact that she was again working with her mentor, Martin Ritt. Creatively, they were a strong team and generally on the same wavelength. Their sense of simpatico was obvious to everyone. In a *New York Times* interview, Gary DeVore, who wrote the screenplay for *Back Roads,* summed up the chemistry between the veteran director and his feisty young star: "He's an old, gray-haired Jew and she's a short, brown-haired *shiksa,* yet Sally and Marty are the same person in a great many ways." According to DeVore, what they shared in common was a mutual lack of ego. For both, the first concern was the project. They just wanted to make the film as good as possible. That was far more important than making themselves look good.

But their friendship didn't begin in the rehearsal hall and end in an editing booth. For Sally, the relationship encompassed far more than just the process of filmmaking, exciting though that was. It became a kind of awakening for her. As she began socializing with Martin Ritt and his wife Adele, and they drew her into their stimulating circle of friends, her interests began to broaden considerably. The Ritts traveled in an urbane, intellectual world, and conversation at their parties went far beyond the latest proposed merger between Avco/Embassy and United Artists. The talk was far more likely to include art, politics, and philosophy. Sally, who'd never gone to college and admittedly wasn't very well read or well traveled, suddenly found herself eager to learn. Under the Ritts' influence, she discovered a wealth of authors—and ideas—that gave her a whole new perspective on life.

Unfortunately, *Back Roads* didn't turn out to be a triumphant encore for Sally Field and Martin Ritt. CBS Theatrical Films had pumped eight million dollars into the production and even rushed to release it before the end of 1980, hoping it would garner at least a few Oscar nominations. But the film drew only lukewarm responses from audiences and critics alike. *Variety* called it "a love story, with humor, about a man and woman brought together by hardship who dream of making a better life," but *Us* magazine dismissed the movie as "a combination of *The Lower Depths* and *It Happened One Night.*"

Sally's appearance in *Back Roads* may have actually been to the film's detriment. Moviegoers, it seemed, weren't eager to accept her as a girl of the streets. In his review of the film, Rex Reed wrote, "Sally Field is one of the freshest, most appealing, energetic, and gifted young actresses on the screen today. But cast her as a broken-down prostitute and you're asking the audience to believe Mt. Fuji is part of the Blue Ridge Mountains."

If the film had won a few Academy Award nominations, business at the box office might have picked up, but Oscar completely passed it by. Even the Best Actress category was a lockout. With performers like Sissy Spacek (*Coal Miner's Daughter*), Mary Tyler Moore (*Ordinary People*), and Goldie Hawn (*Private Benjamin*), Sally barely stood out in the crowd and didn't get a nomination. One year after making *Norma Rae*, she seemed no further along in her career than before.

If anything, she was actually moving backward. According to Sally, most of the scripts she now received were "garbage"—and even if a screenplay attracted her, for one reason or another it never got made. It was almost as if winning the Oscar had left her jinxed. In general, 1980 and 1981 were bleak years indeed.

There was talk of Sally starring in *The Sleepwalker*, where she'd play a character whose astral dreams start to take control of her life, but that screenplay never got off the ground. Sally was also rumored to be up for the part of Luciano Pavarotti's co-star in *Yes, Giorgio*, but the film was ultimately made with newcomer Kathryn Harrold, not Sally, sharing the screen with the famed opera singer.

Things started looking up again when Sally was signed by the Rastar organization to star in *No Small Affair*, her third film for Martin Ritt. The script appealed to her right off the bat. This time she'd be playing a faded New York nightclub singer who becomes romantically involved with a fifteen-year-old high-school student. Matthew Broderick, who'd later emerge as a full-fledged teen idol in *War Games*, was set to play Sally's adolescent love interest. Moreover, with this film (which Columbia had agreed to release) Sally would finally achieve superstar status. Her salary would be a cool million.

Budgeted at nine million dollars, *No Small Affair* went into production on March 9, 1981, but it was doomed from the start. The cameras had barely started rolling when Martin Ritt began suffering from severe—and increasing—bouts of exhaustion. Apparently, Ritt had been ailing ever since working on *Back Roads* the previous summer (the Texas heat and Tommy Lee Jones's temperament had just been too much for him). Every day Ritt appeared to be a little more tired. Finally, after three weeks of filming in midtown Manhattan and Greenwich Village, Ritt was too ill to continue working. Rastar was forced to shut down production indefinitely. Rumors that the sixty-two-year-old director had suffered a heart attack were vigorously denied, but he did require complete rest for some time.

At first Rastar toyed with the idea of salvaging the film. They tried hiring another "name" director to take over the project, but didn't have much luck. The only director who expressed interest was Mark Rydell, and he came part-and-parcel with a scheduling conflict: Rydell was already committed to another project. He wanted to postpone working on *No Small Affair* until he finished *On Golden Pond*. That would have meant starting over from scratch, bcause of the weather factor. Ritt's scenes had been shot in winter (when Manhattan was still covered with snow) and Rydell wouldn't be ready to start until summer (when the snow would be long gone). There was no way to make Ritt's scenes and Rydell's scenes match. If Rydell took over the picture, it would cost an extra two million dollars to reshoot everything that Ritt had already done. (At the same time, threats of a simultaneous directors' and writers' strike were also making the studio very nervous.) So, in the midst of all these considerations, Rastar and Columbia decided to abandon the film. Once again Sally's career had taken another bad turn. (In 1984 *No Small Affair* was actually made, but with different leads. Jon Cryer and Demi Moore played the roles originally intended for Matthew Broderick and Sally Field; Jerry Schatzberg directed.)

But *No Small Affair* wasn't the only project that blew up in Sally's face. There was also talk of co-starring her with Richard Dreyfuss in a film called *Mixed Feelings*. That would have reunited Sally with Irving Ravetch and Harriet Frank Jr., but it all came to naught. And the same fate awaited the script of a movie called *Revelation*. Jack Clayton—best known for the Simone Signoret/Laurence Harvey film, *Room at the Top*—was slated to direct. The role might have been Sally's biggest challenge yet (and quite a change of pace after *Back Roads*). Her character was going to be a thirty-six-year-old virgin who felt emotionally stifled living in a small religious community. But it never came to pass.

After the cancellation of *Revelation*—and all the other setbacks—Sally was beginning to feel a bit like the character she never got to play . . . as if her career didn't have a prayer.

11. A Long Way From Home

In the midst of all these false starts, there was one bright note: Director Sydney Pollack, whose screen successes included *They Shoot Horses, Don't They* and *The Electric Horseman*, wanted Sally to star in his new movie, *Absence of Malice*. She immediately said yes.

The screenplay, written by Kurt Luedtke, a former news reporter, focused on the tragic conflict that arises when the public's right to know directly interferes with an individual's right to privacy. Sally's character, Megan Carter, is an investigative reporter for a top Miami newspaper. In her rush to gain a front-page byline, she mistakenly implicates a mobster's nephew in a gangland-style murder, then makes an even more damning miscalculation trying to clear his name in print. Checking out his alibi, she learns that he spent the night of the murder helping a friend (played by Melinda Dillon) obtain an abortion. Megan prints that information with the highest motives in mind, hoping it will exonerate a man she has previously libeled. Instead, the girl whose personal life she has now laid bare commits suicide.

The moment Sally read the script, she felt Megan Carter

was a character she had to play. To make the project even more tempting, Sydney Pollack began lining up an equally impressive cast. The first order of business was finding a co-star for Sally. Pollack was hoping to sign Al Pacino as the falsely maligned businessman who becomes Megan's conscience and nemesis, as well as her lover, and the chemistry between them might have been interesting indeed. But Pacino was unavailable because of another commitment. He was already signed to appear on-stage in New Haven, Connecticut, in *American Buffalo*. After losing Pacino, Pollack turned to Paul Newman, who was eager to do the role and free to begin filming at once.

Sally was particularly excited about working with Newman, who was another longtime favorite of her friend Martin Ritt. Marty had nothing but praise for Newman's talent and professionalism, although he did warn Sally to be on guard. Newman—a prankster par excellence—was famous for pulling well-orchestrated gags on his unsuspecting co-stars. Sally could expect to find her script and her chair missing once in a while, and if that's all that ever happened, she'd be lucky. She might get her shoes nailed to the floor, too! Ritt knew whereof he spoke: Ritt and Newman had collaborated on several films, including *Hud, Hombre,* and *The Outrage*.

Aside from Field, Newman, and Melinda Dillon—a Broadway and screen actress of some note—the distinguished cast also included Bob Balaban as a duplicitous government investigator and Wilford Brimley as another government agent, who appears in the last few reels to adroitly disentangle the mountain of legal (and illegal) subterfuges that Sally Field and Paul Newman have perpetrated on one another.

From the beginning, there was a touch of irony surrounding the making of *Absence of Malice*. Director Pollack opted for a closed set, which meant no reporters or photographers were allowed to watch any of the filming in progress. Was he worried that the press would perpetrate the same kind of journalistic abuses that were being examined in Luedtke's screenplay?

Chances are, Pollack was more concerned about the press not getting too close a glimpse of his somewhat difficult leading lady. Sally, whose private relationship with Burt Reynolds was practically in its death throes at that point, was earning a reputation for being imperious on the set. She was obviously exhausted from her weekend jaunts from Miami to Atlanta (where Burt was on location) and there were other pressures, too. She hated being away from her children, she felt uncomfortable around Newman, who was somewhat overbearing, and she was no longer one-hundred percent pleased with the script.

She had good reason to worry about how her character was coming across on-screen. As the film developed, it became more and more apparent that Newman's character, not Sally's, was emerging as the more sympathetic figure of the two. The turning point in the script came when Melinda Dillon's character committed suicide as a result of Sally's reckless journalistic revelations. From that point on, it became increasingly difficult to identify with Sally at all. A definite shift took place, making Newman the true protagonist of the film. Pollack even allowed a highly controversial scene, in which an enraged Newman physically attacks Sally, to remain in the final version. Interestingly enough, audiences weren't appalled at seeing Paul Newman, the beloved matinee idol, mistreat a woman on-screen. In this case, they felt Sally deserved it.

All in all, Sally's character really got the short end of the stick. After allowing Megan Carter to indulge in some questionable journalistic grandstanding, the screenwriter then let her compromise her professional ethics in an even more dangerous way. She embarked on a romance with Newman, the man she was supposed to be investigating. Another actress might have refused to play a role with so many barbed edges. Sally had her doubts, too, but was consistently overruled by Pollack and the producer. Ultimately, she made her peace with Megan Carter, and even defended that romantic plot twist on the basis of its entertainment value. (Obviously moviegoers would have been disappointed if Sally Field and Paul Newman had never kissed on-screen.) "We weren't making a movie about the newspaper business," Sally emphatically declared. "You want people to come see the movie and one thing that people like is romance."

Off-screen, Sally's relationship with Newman was nothing approaching even platonic hugs and kisses. It was actually lukewarm to cool, despite the fact that she'd had such a warm rapport with his wife, Joanne Woodward, on the TV-movie *Sybil*. The trouble was, Sally felt like an outsider on the film. Paul Newman, Sydney Pollack, and producer Ron Schwary were like three old college buddies. Pollack had directed Newman's good friend Robert Redford in two movies, *Three Days of the Condor* and *The Electric Horseman*, so the two of them could easily sit around for hours on end just discussing the great gags they'd both played on Redford in the past. Later on, reminiscing in *McCall's* about her sense of being odd-girl-out on the *Malice* set, Sally said, "They'd tell funny stories about things they did on other films, and their practical jokes never stopped. I really didn't fit in, but I did laugh a lot."

On movie sets where actors are virtually "snowed in" with each other for weeks on end, they usually invent some diversion—marathon poker, gin rummy, even taking bets on who'll come down with the first case of "Montezuma's Revenge"—to keep them all from going stir-crazy. These frenetic, nonstop tension-breakers serve as the glue that binds them together for the duration of their mutual imprisonment. On *Absence of Malice* a very special pastime developed: the ritual of the nightly cook-off.

Both Paul Newman and Sydney Pollack considered themselves better-than-average cooks (certainly they both had bigger-than-average culinary egos), and every night they'd try to outdo each other preparing elaborate meals. (The contest really got out of hand when they started having gourmet ingredients flown in from New York and Los Angeles.) And poor Sally had to be the judge, a position she certainly didn't relish. She later recalled that she felt like a Supreme Court justice diplomatically trying to worm her way out of offending anyone. One night she'd praise Paul's spicy chicken recipe; the next night she'd rave about Sydney's exotic chili. Sometimes she felt so agitated from trying to arbitrate their crazy culinary war that what she really longed for was Pepto Bismol!

After a while, Sally started making excuses—she was too tired, she had so many letters to write, etc. etc. etc.—every time her meringue-mad director or her soufflé-happy leading man invited her to dine in his aromatic dressing trailer. She'd quietly sneak back to her own trailer and fix herself something simple, a hamburger or an omelet. Of course, eventually Sally had to reciprocate and invite the Gruesome Gourmet Twosome over for dinner, too. No young bride preparing to feed her stone-faced mother-in-law for the first time could have been more intimidated. Sally decided to barbecue some chicken—that seemed safe enough—but it turned out to be a tension-filled experience. Newman began criticizing her poultry credentials from the moment he arrived. He reprimanded her for not waiting to cook the chicken until the charcoals were white-hot—and when he saw the bottle of cheap Soave that she'd innocently set out on the table, he was disappointed to say the least. Newman, a self-appointed wine connoisseur, launched into a long dissertation on all the creative wine choices that Sally might have made to truly complement the main course.

Is it any wonder that Sally Field and Paul Newman never worked together on another film after *Absence of Malice*? Some silver-haired matinee idols, she discovered, are better off worshipped from afar.

The movie opened around the country in December 1981, just in time for Academy Award consideration. The reviews were excellent, and the long lines at the box office even more encouraging. Suddenly Sally was enjoying her biggest artistic success since *Norma Rae,* and her biggest commercial success since her four-picture comedy fling with Burt Reynolds. Not a bad comeback at all.

When the Academy Award nominations were announced, Paul Newman received his fifth Best Actor nod and Melinda Dillion managed to grab a slot for herself in the Supporting Actress category. In another year, when the competition was less stiff, Sally might have been a Best Actress contender, but 1981 turned out to be a year brimming with notable female performances. The five Best Actress nominees were Katharine Hepburn (*On Golden Pond*), Diane Keaton (*Reds*), Marsha Mason (*Only When I Laugh*), Susan Sarandon (*Atlantic City*), and Meryl Streep (*The French Lieutenant's Woman*). Even Sissy Spacek (*Raggedy Man*), Candice Bergen (*Rich and Famous*), and Faye Dunaway (*Mommie Dearest*) were left off the list.

Sally was only half disappointed. She realized that Megan Carter's semi-likability might account, at least partially, for her being denied an Oscar nomination. Indeed, over the years, very few villains and antiheroes have even come close to fondling the coveted gold statuette. Self-sacrificing maternal types—from Joan Crawford in *Mildred Pierce* right down to Meryl Streep in *Sophie's Choice*—are still Oscar's perennial pets. Winning actresses don't necessarily have to play saints, as long as there's something innately lovable about them. Even if the character is a prostitute (Elizabeth Taylor, *Butterfield 8*) or a convicted murderer (Susan Hayward, *I Want to Live*), it's okay as long as the audience is still on her side. But in Sally's case, the audience sympathy just wasn't there.

To a certain extent, though, the very contrariness of misguided Megan Carter was a turn-on. Sally liked the challenge itself, the idea of playing a woman who was responsible for destroying one man's career and another woman's life. "I thought it was interesting to play someone who doesn't necessarily have the audience on her side, rooting her on," Sally explained to Wayne Warga of *The Los Angeles Times* on the eve of the Oscar nominations. "It's real scary right now waiting to see if it works."

Even without that nomination, Sally had little reason to complain. Overall, in terms of her career, this film was a giant step forward, for Sally got a chance to display a totally different side of her talent. This time she was playing a professional woman, a character who was bright, educated and independent—and on one level at least, Megan Carter represented the woman that Sally herself had striven so hard to become during the last decade.

Playing a reporter was no problem, either. Unlike some celebrities, Sally had always enjoyed a friendly, open relationship with the press. At times she may have bridled at some of the headlines about her romance with Burt Reynolds, but on the whole she was generally forthright and cooperative when it came to dealing with reporters. She regularly granted interviews to *Redbook, Ladies' Home Journal, McCall's,* and *Playgirl.* Sally was a delightful subject— she always felt comfortable being interviewed. Even back in her days as a fresh-faced teenager on "Gidget" and "The Flying Nun," she'd been just as open with magazines like *Photoplay* and *Modern Screen.* In fact, Sally made such unerringly honest copy that for a long time she helped keep some of those fan publications in business.

Still and all, once *Absence of Malice* was done, Sally was glad to move on. Interestingly enough, for some reason she didn't seek out another modern professional woman to play. Instead, as she invariably did, she returned to her own Southern roots and chose something much simpler. Sally enjoyed playing country women with a lot of fire in their eyes behind those bland, plaintive smiles. She never gravitated toward the Blanche DuBois and Maggie the Cat kind of roles, the neurotic Tennessee Williams heroines who were better left to the likes of Elizabeth Taylor and Geraldine Page. Sally latched on to a less celebrated—and more optimistic—kind of Southern woman: the hard-working, homespun survivor. It was a portrait that came much closer to the women in her own family. Her decision to accept a leading role in a new stage production of Tad Mosel's gently poetic play *All The Way Home* was a welcome opportunity to satisfy just that need in her.

The original Broadway drama, based on James Agee's novel *A Death in the Family,* had won critical acclaim and a well-deserved Pulitzer Prize in 1961. Two years later, the film version, starring Jean Simmons and Robert Preston, had also earned kudos. The story, set in 1910, was an introspective look at a rural family forced to deal with the untimely death of a young husband and provider. The script followed their lives both before and after the tragic event. In this new production, which would be staged in the Bing Theater at the University of Southern California (and simultaneously televised live on NBC), William Hurt was cast as the young husband who dies in an automobile accident, and Sally was to portray his widow, a woman forced to hold her family together in the wake of overwhelming circumstances. The admirable supporting cast included Ned Beatty, Ellen Corby, Murray Hamilton, Polly Holliday, and Jeanette Nolan.

"It's a more tragic role than I have ever played," Sally confided to Cecil Smith of *The Los Angeles Times,* but she noted parallels to her own family background. Sally had been raised in a house where, until Jock Mahoney's arrival on the scene, a male influence had been totally lacking. Her own father had walked out; grandfathers and uncles were in short supply. So she fully understood the plight of Mary Follet, the character she was about to play in *All the Way Home.* Recalling her own childhood, she remarked, "I had lots of family around me, all women—the men were dead or gone or something. I had my Aunt Gladys, my Aunt Pearl, my grandmother Joy, my great-grandmother Minnie—all Southern women. They were Southerners transplanted to the San Fernando Valley. I could identify with Mary Follet the moment I read this script."

This stage/TV production of *All the Way Home* turned out to be one of Sally's most satisfying triumphs. It was her first major performance on television since *Sybil* in 1976, and she hoped to be able to return to the small screen in the future to do more projects of the same caliber. Although Sally would never consider resuming the grind of a weekly series—or even reverting to the kind of slapdash Movies of the Week that had occupied her in the early 1970s—she certainly wouldn't mind immersing herself in truly quality work on television.

Meanwhile, Sally continued to plug away at her roller-coaster movie career. In 1982 she embarked on a comedy film, *Kiss Me Goodbye,* which paired her with Jeff Bridges (her old *Stay Hungry* leading man) and James Caan. The movie, which was basically a remake of the 1978 Brazilian import *Dona Flor and Her Two Husbands,* related the charmingly absurd story of a woman torn between two lovers— one alive and one dead. Representing the flesh-and-blood world was the dull but likable suitor obsessed with marrying her. From beyond the grave came her mischievous late husband (looking remarkably well for one so lifeless) whose only mission on earth, it seemed, was to meddle in his wife's affairs. Jeff Bridges played the bumbling new bridegroom-to-be, while James Caan was cast as the talkative corpse.

Obviously, plotwise all this was rather thin stuff to begin with. But *Kiss Me Goodbye* suffered further from critical comparison to the Brazilian original, which had quietly become a long-running hit on the art-film circuit. Released shortly before the end of 1982, *Kiss Me Goodbye* proved to be one of Sally's least successful efforts. It sputtered fitfully at the box office and was quickly forgotten. (It was later resurrected on cable TV, where it did substantially better.)

Ironically, at the same time that *Kiss Me Goodbye* was gasping for life in movie theaters, Sally's former other half— Burt Reynolds—was mired down in ticket-sales problems of his own. His latest film, *Best Friends,* a romantic comedy that paired him with funny girl Goldie Hawn, wasn't exactly setting box-office records, either. Strange how fate has a way of writing ironic postscripts to some stories, isn't it? Hollywood observers couldn't help noting that, when it came to comedy at least, maybe Burt and Sally were better off together than apart. Neither of them seemed able to find the same natural, seemingly effortless chemistry with another movie partner. (Amazingly enough, Sally would fare best of all on-screen in her next film, *Places of the Heart,* where she'd be surrounded by three talented character actors—John Malkovich, Ed Harris, and Danny Glover—and no leading man at all.)

Well, if Sally wasn't making cinema history in the man department, her personal life wasn't in much better shape. In 1982, a year after severing the golden cord with Burt Reynolds, she was still basically alone. And being alone was something she had never really come to terms with. It was a condition she merely endured, not one she cultivated and relished.

That point was resoundingly brought home to her when she set off for Europe—for the first time—to help promote *Absence of Malice,* which was scheduled to open in several overseas markets. Over there, her loneliness became excruciating. Far from home and family—and feeling claustrophobic in all those neat-as-a-pin, but strangely unwelcoming hotel rooms—she would run away from her "aloneness" as fast as she could and haunt friendly pubs and bistros at night. The woman sitting in those smoky, dimly lit places was hardly the Sally Field that anyone in Los Angeles might have recognized. There she was, elaborately coiffed and dressed, smoking and drinking, sitting at a table all by herself, and trying to look appropriately blasé. She always carried a copy of Will Durant's *Story of Philosophy* with her. It kept her company everywhere she went, and yet she never finished reading even the first chapter. Apparently, Sally hungered for something more than could be found between the pages of a book.

She was hungry for fulfillment—not for sexual adventures (she never allowed herself to get picked up in any of those bars), not for glamor, not even for kicks, but for something much deeper than that. She simply wanted a partner, a companion, a soulmate—a man whose life would be permanently and comfortably entwined with hers. Sitting in cafés in Rome and Paris, thousands of miles from home, Sally realized just how *settled* she really needed to be.

Ever since she was a young girl, Sally had kept a journal, a diary of her most intimate thoughts and feelings. It had followed her all through her "Gidget" years right down to Burt Reynolds, *Norma Rae,* and Martin Ritt. In 1982, when she was rushing through Europe all alone and indulging her *Blue Angel* fantasies every night, Sally invented a new persona for herself. In her journal she began calling herself Genevieve—it sounded just right to go with the slightly decadent, pseudo-expatriate pose she was trying so hard to effect. Was that why she created Genevieve? Partially. But mainly Sally needed the shelter of a sophisticated new alter ego—a temporary fantasy friend—because of the emptiness and the pain she felt in her own life.

No matter how rich or adored or successful she became, she was still—in the last analysis—a long way from home.

12. "You Like Me! . . . You Really Like Me!"

Looking back on her twenty-year career in films and television, Sally Field has no trouble pinpointing the high spots. On only three occasions, she believes, has she portrayed characters who truly tested her mettle as an actress. She considers those characters "my best work." She views the opportunity to create those women as rare and perfect situations where "the work and the actress have been indistinguishable."

It's not hard to figure out which screen roles she's referring to. Obviously, the first two incarnations were Sybil and Norma Rae. The third character was Edna Spaulding, the courageous farm woman she played in the 1984 film *Places in the Heart*. That role reaffirmed Sally's reputation as one of the most dynamic dramatic actresses in America, and it culminated in her winning a second Academy Award.

In a sense, it erased (or at least shoved into the background) all the artistic and commercial failures she'd endured since *Norma Rae*, from selling out in *Beyond the Poseidon Adventure* to bombing out in *Back Roads* and *Kiss*

133

Me Goodbye. Suddenly, five years after Hollywood had first put her on a pedestal and then quickly allowed her to slip off, Sally Field was back on top again.

Her comeback film had the same kind of tender loving care in its creation and execution that Martin Ritt and his screenwriting team had put into *Norma Rae*. *Places in the Heart* was written and directed by Robert Benton, one of Hollywood's most respected new filmmakers. Although Sally had never crossed paths with him before, he was hardly a stranger to her. In fact, she remembered his name vividly from the 1980 Oscar telecast. That year, while she was being honored for her performance in *Norma Rae,* Benton scored a double victory with *Kramer vs. Kramer*. He went home with an Oscar tucked under each arm—one for directing and one for adapting Avery Corman's novel to the screen.

This film, set in a small Texas town in the 1930s, was something of a family memoir for writer-director Benton. Much of the script incorporated elements of Benton's own Depression-era childhood in Waxahachie, Texas; and the central character, Edna Spaulding—a young widow struggling against all odds to hold on to her failing cotton farm and keep her family from being split up—bore a striking resemblance to Benton's grandmother. In the opening scene of *Places in the Heart,* Edna's husband, the local sheriff, is killed while on a routine patrol. Benton's own grandfather had been shot and killed under similar circumstances, just four days before Christmas in Waxahachie.

As with all her best work, Sally knew at once that the role was a gem—and too good to pass up. If need be, she was all set to beg, plead, bully, or argue to get the role, but fortunately Robert Benton didn't need much convincing. He was a Sally Field fan of long standing and had pretty much already decided that no other actress could play Edna Spaulding half as well. And this time Sally didn't need Burt Reynolds's assurance (or anyone else's, for that matter) to tell her she was making the right decision. "I read twenty pages [of the script] and my hands were trembling," she later told Jeff Silverman of *The Chicago Tribune*. "I knew it was simply the best script that I had ever read."

Well, Benton may have believed that she was far and away the best actress for the role, but Sally was a little less optimistic. If she could only convince herself of the same thing. The script seemed positively brilliant to her. Could she possibly live up to the quality of the material—and Benton's high-toned expectations for her? "The fear," she said, "is that *you* won't be as good as *it* [the material] is. That *you'll* let it down."

Unlike some films that spend ten or fifteen minutes cinematically setting the mood (while the audience finishes buying popcorn and finding seats), *Places in the Heart* built swiftly to a heart-wrenching emotional pitch. It began with the death of Edna's husband and homed right in on the sense of loss, shock, and isolation that immediately engulfed the whole family. From there, it focused on the next crucial year of her life—Edna's battle to save both her farm (from the local bank) and her children (from becoming wards of the county). The script followed her alternate bouts of ingenuity and despair as she tried to raise a successful cotton crop, her only hope of avoiding foreclosure. Helping her in her practically impossible task were an itinerant black field hand (Danny Glover) and a blind boarder (John Malkovich). As a team, a more compelling trio of underdogs had rarely been encountered on-screen.

Meanwhile, a bittersweet subplot centered on Edna's sister (Lindsay Crouse), her philandering husband (Ed Harris), and an overly friendly neighbor (Amy Madigan). The racial issue—an important part of that time and place—was woven into the plot, too, with Danny Glover's character being brutally terrorized by the local Ku Klux Klan.

In creating the character of Edna Spaulding, Sally had a wealth of carefully preserved stories and memories to draw on from the Southern farm women in her own family. But even if Sally's roots had been Boston Brahmin or Bronx Jewish instead, it would have been hard—indeed, practically impossible—to strike a false note in this role. There was something so universal about Edna's plight—about her economic and spiritual struggle to survive—that it easily struck a responsive chord in Sally. She found herself comparing the obstacles and hardships that Edna faced to some of the bleak moments in her own life.

Like Edna Spaulding, Sally knew all about the subtle terrors of running a household alone, of trying to be both breadwinner and hearth-tender, without a man to help shoulder the burden. Like Edna, she was a woman with a mortgage to pay and two children to support, forced to rely on her own resources. And like Edna—who frequently felt angry and frustrated confronting unsympathetic bankers and unscrupulous cotton dealers—Sally herself had been victimized by the male power structure on more than one occasion. Were Hollywood picture-makers much better than Dustbowl cotton traders when it came to dealing with women? Sally could count on her fingers the number of times she'd been done in by the blatantly paternalistic attitudes of chauvinistic producers, directors, and studio executives. How well she identified with Edna's unspoken rage at men who gallantly claimed to be protecting her best interests even while they glibly shortchanged and cheated her.

But Benton's movie was a poetic character study of one woman's life, not a political diatribe on the theme of women's rights. Women's rights was hardly a subject that would have occuped Edna Spaulding's thoughts anyway, so Sally's first task was to separate Edna's anger from her own. They were two different women living in two different worlds. Edna Spaulding, a rural, church-going housewife of the 1930s, hardly coveted the same kind of independence that Sally Field, a high-powered, goal-oriented career woman of the 1980s, required to feel happy and fulfilled. To try to turn Edna Spaulding into some sort of Depression-era spokeswoman for women's liberation would have been false and misleading. As Sally explained to reporter Jeff Silverman, "I had to make sure that even when she got stronger or more capable of dealing with the outside world, that she never left 1935. . . ."

On location in Waxahachie, Sally (ever true to her Method instincts) quickly immersed herself in Edna's world. In fact, she became so emotionally caught up in the inner turmoil of the character she was playing that at times it was difficult to step back. In preparing for the scene where Edna learns of her husband's death, Sally worked herself up to a fever pitch before she ever got in front of the camera. She sank into a silent depression that totally drained her. Then, fearing that the crew would think she was either drunk or demented, she decided she couldn't face anyone on the set. She sat for hours all alone on the front porch of Edna's farmhouse, quietly crying. Luckily, she had a director who not only understood her strange method of acting, but actually appreciated the contribution it would ultimately make to her performance. So Benton considerately held up filming and waited patiently for Sally to collect herself.

Finally, Lindsay Crouse, who was playing her sister, walked onto the porch and sat down next to her. Lindsay didn't say a word. She just sat there, holding Sally's hand and stroking her hand. "She was really being my sister," Sally later said. "I must have sat there and cried for two hours. Then we walked onto the set and did our scene."

Sally put that same kind of intensity into her entire performance, and it paid off. Every scene of hers was perfectly crafted. If anything, she gave Robert Benton so many moving and beautiful moments to choose from that his only problem, during post-production, was editing down the footage to a reasonable length. Ultimately he did, and when it premiered, *Places in the Heart* didn't disappoint anyone. It opened to unanimously favorable reviews that ran the gamut from glowing to magnificent. *New York Times* movie critic Vincent Canby called *Places in the Heart* "one of the best films in years about growing up American."

The film received several Academy Award nominations including Best Picture (it lost to *Amadeus*). Benton was nominated for both direction and writing (and won his third Oscar for the film's original screenplay); Sally was nominated for Best Actress, and John Malkovich and Lindsay Crouse were both nominated for their supporting roles.

It seemed like history was repeating itself when the nominees were announced in February 1985. Once again—just as with *Norma Rae*—Sally was considered the favorite to walk off with Best Actress honors. Ironically, two of her strongest competitors in this year's Oscar race—Jessica Lange (*Country*) and Sissy Spacek (*The River*)—were both under consideration for very similar roles. Each had played an indomitable farm woman faced with foreclosure and bankruptcy, but for some reason neither of their performances had generated quite as much heat as Sally's. (Besides, both were recent Oscar winners.) The final two nominees, both British actresses, were considered long shots. They were Judy Davis, for her part as a stubborn young Englishwoman in David Lean's production of *A Passage to India,* and Vanessa Redgrave for her portrayal of a 19th-century feminist in *The Bostonians,* based on the Henry James classic and directed by James Ivory.

In winning a second Academy Award, Sally was now guaranteed an enviable place in Oscar history. Only a select group of actresses—among them Katharine Hepburn, Bette Davis, Vivien Leigh, Genda Jackson, and Jane Fonda—had ever been awarded more than one Oscar in the Best Actress category. On Oscar night 1985, Sally's excitement was justifiably unparalleled.

Her acceptance speech, which later drew much laughter and criticism, reflected her unbridled state of euphoria. When she stood at the podium, nervously clutching her Oscar and facing an audience of tuxedo-clad film execs and bejeweled box-office sirens, Sally wildly babbled, "I wanted more than anything else to have your respect . . . and I can't deny the fact that you like me—right now. You like me!"

What in the world had prompted Sally to gush like an overenthusiastic schoolgirl? Nervousness, perhaps. Shock, too. (This time she truly hadn't expected to win.) She later defended her remarks by commenting that "I merely said what was in my heart."

If so, then the key word in Sally's rambling speech had to be *respect.* Everything else hinged on that. In Sally's mind, the fact that Hollywood was willing to give her another Oscar meant that *Norma Rae* hadn't been a fluke—her movie-industry peers had finally, truly accepted her as a serious actress. They no longer viewed her as just Burt Reynolds's girlfriend or a tired-out TV star foolishly trying to recycle her talent on the movie screen.

And this time she wouldn't make the same mistakes that had followed in the wake of her first Oscar. This time there would be no more *Poseidon* misadventures.

13. Second Chances

If *Places in the Heart* gave Sally Field a second chance on the professional front, it also brought about a far more startling change in her personal life. It coaxed her out of her shell.

In the four years since she'd broken up with Burt Reynolds, Sally had literally gone out of her way not to get seriously involved with any man. Why put herself through all that pain? Considering her track record in the romance department, she had good reason to be leery of sharing her life again.

But during the months she spent in Waxahachie, far away from the celebrity glare of Los Angeles, something happened. While she was all wrapped up in Robert Benton's script, developing and refining the character of Edna Spaulding, a catharsis took place. Maybe it was the change of scenery, or the role she was playing, or both. At any rate, the more she studied Edna's world, the more she came to an inescapable conclusion: Something vital was sadly missing in her own life. Despite the fact that Edna was a simple farm woman, she possessed something crucial that Sally lacked— the ability to reach out to other people. Edna wasn't afraid to love, and Sally now realized she didn't want to be either.

Yet for so long she'd gone to such monumental lengths to deny it. After walking out on Burt, Sally had gone around telling herself, "I don't want anybody! I don't need anybody!" It was as though she had never stopped playing Megan Carter, the self-sufficient, self-involved professional woman in *Absence of Malice*. But her emotionally exhausting—and yet strangely uplifting—experience making *Places in the Heart* changed all that. "Playing Edna Spaulding opened me up," Sally said. "I rediscovered the fact that people are meant to need each other."

Not that Sally had condemned herself to living the life of a nun. Far from it. It was just that much of the time, she'd felt more like a bystander than a participant as far as her romantic life was concerned.

All her post-Burt relationships were casual and transitory. Sally, for instance, had made rather sensational headlines with TV talk-host Johnny Carson, who courted her right after the breakup of his third marriage. The press had a field day with the fact that Carson was nearly old enough to be Sally's father and that the two of them refused to pose for photographs together. Probably that was more Johnny's style than Sally's. He was still reeling from the steamy public disclosures that had surfaced during his divorce and alimony battles with his ex-wife Joanna.

During her involvement with Johnny, what appealed to Sally was his sense of humor and his sense of power. In some ways, he reminded her of Burt. Here was a man who could call his own shots in Hollywood. He had reached such a high level of success that NBC kowtowed to him and not vice versa. It reminded her very much of Burt Reynolds's position with the major movie studios. Because of his ultra-successful track record at the box office, Burt could negotiate just about any kind of contract he wanted.

But Johnny Carson, like Burt, was hardly a candidate for a permanent involvement, and Sally soon moved on to actor Kevin Kline, who was much closer to her own age. Now the tables were reversed professionally, for Sally was the far more established star of the two. Kline, who'd recently won a Tony Award for his performance in the Broadway musical *The Pirates of Penzance,* was just starting to make a name for himself on the motion-picture scene. In his very first movie—a spectacular debut—he played Meryl Streep's lover in *Sophie's Choice.* Then he went on to give another acclaimed performance as Glenn Close's husband in *The Big Chill.*

Kline, however, didn't prove any more durable a fixture in Sally's life than Johnny Carson had. She later confessed that the fault was probably hers. At the time she was dating him, she knew she was giving off "leave-me-alone vibes." Nothing would have frightened Sally more than a serious discussion of marriage, likable though Kline was. Eventually he got the message and moved on.

Then, early in 1984, movie producer Alan Greisman entered the picture—or, to be more precise, reentered it. Sally had first noticed him two years before when, coincidentally, they'd been lunching at the same restaurant. She couldn't help catching his eye, and even then Sally had been intrigued enough by Greisman's good looks and pleasant smile to casually ask her lunch partner, "Who is that attractive man across the room?"

But nothing came of it. All through that brief restaurant encounter Sally had kept surreptitiously glancing at him—and she knew he was glancing at her, too. Still, neither of them seemed to have the courage or inclination to pursue the situation. She thought about him a bit that afternoon, but by the end of the day she'd put him out of her mind—permanently. Or so she thought.

Fate had something else in mind. Early in 1984, right after Sally had finished work on *Places in the Heart,* Greisman unexpectedly reentered her life. It was strictly business. He approached her with a motion-picture project. Sally had just started her own production company, and Greisman knew she was looking for suitable film properties to develop. Their first meeting was just a case of your-office-or-mine?—and the talk never got much further along than distribution rights and development deals. But there was a slight undercurrent of awkwardness. Sally immediately remembered him from that brief restaurant flirtation two years before, and Greisman had the same reaction. But neither of them really felt comfortable bringing the subject up.

This time, though, Greisman wasn't going to let Sally slip through his fingers. A day or two after that meeting, he sent her a follow-up letter reiterating the various points they had discussed at their meeting. As a kind of parenthetical P.S., he suggested that they have dinner to discuss the project further.

Greisman, who had grown up in Scarsdale, New York, originally came to California to break into the movie business. He was now a producer of some note. At the age of thirty-seven (he was one year younger than Sally), his track record already included such films as *Heartbeat,* with Nick Nolte, Sissy Spacek, and John Heard, and *Modern Romance,* with Albert Brooks and Kathryn Harrold. (In 1985 he was also associated with producng the Chevy Chase comedy-hit *Fletch.*)

What Sally found particularly appealing about this man was the fact that he combined the best of both worlds. He was part show-business entrepreneur and part middle-class

144

civilian. As a film producer, he could understand Sally's professional problems and ambitions; but he could also identify
with—and share—her aspirations for a quiet, settled life.
And since he was a businessman, not an actor, there was
never any sense of competition between them.

At the time they met, Greisman was coming out of a
period of emotional turmoil himself. He had recently broken
up with Lisa Taylor, a Los Angeles model. In fact, he was
just about ready to dive back into the singles scene when he
crossed paths with Sally. Like Sally, an exclusive relationship
was the last thing on his mind.

Well, so much for last things on their minds. From the
night of their first dinner date, Sally Field and Alan
Greisman became inseparable. The romance progressed
steadily and by the fall of 1984 Sally and Alan were actually
living together. Both her sons responded well to Alan. They
liked having him around and seemed happy with their
mother's choice. Peter had once confided to his mother that
she often acted uncomfortable with some of the other men
she'd dated, but not with Alan. In his presence, she always
seemed genuinely relaxed.

With both her sons giving the romance their seal of approval, Sally and Alan saw no reason to wait. In December
1984—ten years after her divorce from Steve Craig—they
were married at her home in Tarzana, California. It was a
small, low-key, nondenominational ceremony (Greisman is
Jewish), and the only flippant touch was the installation of
doorbell chimes that played "Here Comes the Bride" when
the guests arrived. After exchanging vows, the bride and
groom danced to Beach Boys and Beatles songs from the
1960s—their personal choice—and dined and chatted with
the friends and relatives who'd come to wish them well.

The newlyweds barely had time for a honeymoon before

Sally jumped into her next project, *Murphy's Romance*. Sally was nervous, scared, and at the same time more elated than she'd ever been about her work before—and for good reason: This film was going to be a very special labor of love. For one thing, Sally would be wearing a brand-new hat—Madame Filmmaker. *Murphy's Romance* would be the very first enterprise undertaken by her fledgling production company, Fogwood Films. If the film succeeded, Sally might soon be calling her own shots in the movie industry. She'd finally have the money and clout to make the kind of movies she really wanted to.

But dreams of instantly materializing into another Barbra Streisand or Steven Spielberg weren't all that spurred Sally on. *Murphy's Romance* was going to be a personal high, too. It represented a real reunion for Sally and some very speical people in her life. For starters, it would give her another chance with her old friend Marty Ritt. Although the veteran director was now seventy-one, he was in much better health than at the time he'd been forced to drop out of *No Small Affair,* causing the film to be shelved. Sally knew he could handle the directing reins on this new film. And on top of that, *Murphy's Romance* would actually be a four-way reunion since Irving Ravetch and Harriet Frank Jr.—the *Norma Rae* screenwriters—had been hired to write the script.

The film, which took place in a small Arizona town, was basically a romantic comedy. Sally played a young divorced woman with a twelve-year-old son (Corey Haim) who has just arrived in town and is trying to make a new life for herself. James Garner was cast as her character's unlikely romantic companion: a widowed, slightly oddball pharmacist in his mid-fifties who becomes Sally's benefactor and suitor. Forming the crucial third side of the triangle was

Brian Kerwin as Sally's good-for-nothing ex-husband who tracks her down at her new mailing address, quickly moves in, and proceeds to pull out every cheap trick in the book to try to sideswipe her romance with Garner. (The film, of course, was a comedy, so at the end Garner, not Kerwin, got the girl.)

The film went on location in Florence, Arizona (a small town seventy miles southeast of Phoenix), in February 1985. Unlike the situation that had existed on *Back Roads,* this time the sunshine was brilliant, but not debilitating. For James Garner, the hot desert climate was a particularly welcome change after his last assignment—filming the TV-movie *Heartsounds* in Toronto with Mary Tyler Moore. There the weather had been cold and dismal, and the mood on the set often bleak (Garner played a man who was dying of heart disease). An added aggravation was a fire that had broken out in the Toronto hotel where the *Heartsounds* cast was encamped. Garner and his leading lady, Mary Tyler Moore, had had to flee the hotel—in nothing but bathrobes and bed clothes—in the middle of the night to escape the blaze.

But now Garner was relaxed, rested, and feeling in great shape physically. At the age of fifty-seven, he was actually twenty pounds lighter than he'd been during his days on "The Rockford Files." Moreover, he and Sally had a terrific rapport right from the start. He liked to joke around with the crew, play poker, and start shooting early (at the crack of dawn), so he could finish up early every day—all of which dovetailed nicely with Sally's own style of approaching things.

There was only one minor setback during the crew's whole stay in Florence. Irving Ravetch developed a severe case of food poisoning after dining in nearby Mesa. He later called Mesa "the hell-hole of the Western world," which didn't exactly improve relations between the local residents and the visiting film company, but eventually ruffled feelings were smoothed over on both sides.

Sally herself enjoyed being on location in the back roads of Arizona. "I've always felt a really strong connection with small towns," she told a visiting reporter for *The Los Angeles Times.* "Even though I was born in L.A., I fit in better here." And for the first time in a long time, Emma—the strong-willed (but far from brittle) character she was playing—wasn't someone too directly removed from her own experience. She wasn't a prostitute like Amy Post or a newspaper reporter like Megan Carter or a factory drudge like Norma Rae. Emma was simply an ordinary, modern-day woman (divorced and raising a child) who fell in love with an essentially nice, decent man and wanted nothing more than to spend the rest of her life with him. If that didn't sound like shades of Sally's own recent history, then quite possibly nothing ever would.

Sally had no qualms about owning up to the obvious parallels. "There is [lots of] unabashed Sally in it," she said of her performance as Emma. "It wasn't like any of those other parts where I leave Sally at home and develop mannerisms and walks and a whole emotional life that isn't mine."

But trying to sell Sally Field as Sally Field on-screen wasn't perhaps as good an idea as it had looked. It seemed like history was repeating itself once more. A year after Sally had triumphed in *Norma Rae,* she hit the bottom with *Back Roads.* Now, a year after immense success in *Places of the Heart,* she was only making a whimper, not a bang, at the box office with *Murphy's Romance.* But there was no point in blaming anyone. Neither her performance, nor Garner's, nor even the script, nor Marty Ritt's direction really had much to do with it. The times, which were definitely a-changin', just weren't on *Murphy's* side.

It all had to do with economics. Unfortunately, 1985 wasn't a good year for wholesome movies about mature, sensible adults who don't rush into bed at the very first sign of heavy breathing. Maybe that's because mature, sensible adults were deserting the movie theaters in droves, so how could small films like *Murphy's Romance* hope to succeed?

Actually, movie attendance had been dropping off severely for some time (more and more adults preferred to stay home and rent films to watch on their VCRs). Meanwhile, teenagers, who were now the mainstay of the moviegoing audience, were much more interested in fantasy, food fights, sex and violence—and any combination thereof. After *Mad Max* and MTV, mild, unassuming romantic comedies held no appeal for them. The big films of 1985 were *Back to the Future* (sci-fi soap opera) and *Rambo* (a killing field day). And so despite the marvelous chemistry between James Garner and Sally Field—and the fact that *Murphy's Romance* was viewed by most critics as a charming, thoroughly likable piece of entertainment—it came and went at the box office faster than a speeding laser gun. (Later, though, it picked up considerable steam on the video rental circuit.)

There was one bright spot in all this disappointment. After a twenty-two-year-career in motion pictures, *Murphy's Romance* brought James Garner his very first Oscar nomination. Despite his contribution over the years to a slew of memorable films, including *The Great Escape, The Americanization of Emily,* and *Victor, Victoria,* when it came to nomination balloting, he'd always been ignored by the Motion Picture Academy. Now he was finally being recognized for his fine comic talents. Garner, in fact, was considered a front-runner in the 1985 Best Actor competition, but he faltered just short of the finish line.

Why did he lose? Ultimately, tradition worked against

him. Oscar just doesn't think much of romantic leading men—he never has. Merely examine the record: Look at Cary Grant, Rock Hudson, and Robert Redford, none of whom ever won the acting race. Invariably, Oscar feels more comfortable bestowing his blessings on high drama with a capital H, and that's exactly what happened in 1985. When the votes were counted, the award went to a more self-consciously serious dramatic performance than Garner's more humorous—and entertaining—screen job. The winner was William Hurt, for his portrayal of a doomed transvestite in *Kiss of the Spider Woman*.

Well, maybe if James Garner had worn a skirt in *Murphy's Romance*, he might have had a better chance.

14. Bunny Suits and Business Hats

"I don't believe in luck," Sally Field once said. "I've worked . . . I guess in some ways I was in the right place at the right time. But no one handed anything over to me."

It's true. To a large extent, Sally Field has always made her own "luck" in the movie industry. But like most actresses, the one thing she's always lacked is a feeling of power to protect her talent—and that's the key. As anyone who frequents Spago or the Polo Lounge will tell you, power is still the only real form of currency in Hollywood.

Gradually, Sally Field came to know that, and she also came to believe that her future success in show business would always be precarious unless she became part of the movieland power structure. So in 1984, after finishing up *Places in the Heart,* Sally took the first positive step toward changing her future. She went into partnership with Laura Ziskin, a former associate of Barbra Streisand and producer Jon Peters, and created her own production company, Fogwood Films.

The company's *raison d'être* was to find starring vehicles for Sally Field. In today's movie market, where few decent scripts are written and even fewer actually get made into motion pictures, the independent filmmaking route, for many actors, isn't merely an expensive pastime. It's an act of self-preservation. Without her own production arm, even a two-time Academy Award-winning actress such as Sally Field might easily sit for months or even years waiting for a half-way respectable script to come along. As Sally soberly announced to the press, "You either get into producing or you quit."

When Fogwood Films first opened its doors, Sally and Laura Ziskin occupied an office at 20th Century-Fox. Jane Fonda, who was also running her own independent production company, had an office right across the lot. The two women had never been particularly friendly and, except for a brief backstage chat at the 1980 Oscar telecast (when they'd been fellow nominees), they'd scarcely ever run into each other at the same parties or film premieres. But Jane had once written Sally a fan letter, praising her work in *Sybil* and *Norma Rae,* and now Sally decided it might be worth her while to ask Jane's advice, as one female producer to another.

Jane, after all, had been in the producing game for some time, while Sally was still wet behind the ears. To be perfectly frank, Sally was finding the whole operation more than slightly terrifying. She was totally inexperienced with the whole convoluted, frustrating process of putting a movie deal together—buying the screen rights to a play or novel; hiring a film writer to adapt the darn thing; convincing a movie studio to pump some seed money into the project, not to mention negotiating a development deal, and ultimately—ideally—actually getting the movie cast, costumed, insured, and shot. The rigamarole was overwhelming. If nothing else, Sally hoped Jane Fonda could provide some helpful tips on how to retain her sanity.

The two women met for lunch and talked nonstop for over two hours. Jane immediately sensed Sally's insecurity and put her at ease by recounting some of the failures and frustrations she'd encountered when she first went into the production business. "She couldn't have been kinder," Sally later said. "It was almost as if she was physically hugging me with support, and that's just what I needed."

Jane and Sally kept in touch, although they didn't stay office neighbors very long. Within a year, Sally and Laura Ziskin moved their operation to Columbia Studios, where Sally had a new actor-turned-producer for an office neighbor—Stacey Keach, star of TV's "Mickey Spillane's Mike Hammer" series.

Ironically, once she got totally absorbed in the high-powered world of movie deals, Sally found herself spending more time reading scripts and bidding for them than actually standing in front of the cameras. Occasionally, she had more irons in the fire than she could handle—just like any producer worth her salt.

After making *Murphy's Romance,* Sally didn't lack for new ventures to choose from. She fell in love with a book called *Finder,* the biography of Marilyn Greene, a renowned missing-persons hunter. Greene, who works out of Schenectady, New York, claims to have solved more disappearance cases than any other detective in the United States. Sally thought the role would be a fabulous change of pace, but she wasn't the only actress who managed to sneak an advance peek at preliminary galleys of the book months before it was published. Jessica Lange, Cher, and Jane Fonda all joined in the bidding war, too, and Sally eventually decided to move on to other projects.

She turned her attention to *Home Before Morning*, Lynda Van Devanter's highly controversial and disquieting book about nurses who served in the Vietnam war. With Sally agreeing to star in the proposed film version, Columbia Pictures was willing to invest a whopping $20 million in bringing the book to the screen, but the initial publicity surrounding the project wasn't entirely favorable. Nurses Against Misrepresentation, a group of Colorado nurses headed by Pat Walsh, launched a forceful and impassioned campaign against all attempts to film the book, claiming it unfairly depicted the experiences of American nurses in Vietnam. Walsh called *Home Before Morning*, which shows nurses suffering from psychological burnout as well as alcohol and drug problems, "extraordinarily biased and false." Walsh had written her own, much more sympathetic Vietnam memoir, *Forever Sad the Hearts*, but that had no bearing, she claimed, on her antagonism to *Home Before Morning*. Walsh had already withdrawn her book from film consideration, so there was no conflict of interest in her campaign against Van Devanter's book.

Eventually, though, the outcry died down and, as of January 1987, all signals were reportedly "go" on *Home Before Morning*. In fact, Hollywood observers were already predicting a third Oscar nomination for Sally on the basis of Julian Barry's incredibly moving script. (Barry's previous screen adaptations include *Lenny* for Dustin Hoffman and *The River* for Sissy Spacek.)

At the same time, Sally's production company was also preparing two TV-movies: *Second Heaven*, a novel by *Ordinary People* author Judith Guest, and a video biography of antinuclear activist Dr. Helen Caldicott, one of Sally's personal heroes.

In the interim, while waiting for all these scripts to be readied, Sally joined Michael Caine and Steve Guttenberg in *Surrender,* a film that was destined to be notable for a single choice moment, if for nothing else. At one point in the movie, robbers force Sally to strip naked—her first on-screen disrobing since *Stay Hungry* in 1976.

Amazing as it seems, while other stars in their forties are starting to wind down their careers, Sally continues to quietly move ahead with more projects than ever before. Her durability has certainly surprised a lot of her early detractors. The beachy-keen teenager, who first became a bubbly role-model for clean-cut kids of the 1960s, has now been adopted by a whole new generation—the college kids of the Eighties. In February 1985 Sally was named Woman of the Year by Harvard's Hasty Pudding Theatrical Club (Sylvester Stallone was Man of the Year) and she had the time of her life camping it up with the Hasty Pudding set at a parade in Cambridge held in her honor.

In presenting her with her Hasty Pudding award, the collegians noted that the awards are presented annually to a man and woman who've made "a lasting contribution to the world of entertainment." Sally was cited, in particular, for her rich diversity of roles.

At the dinner that accompanied the parade, Sally had no trouble getting right into the satirical, frat-house spirit of things. When the Hasty Pudding Club presented her with a size 48D brassiere, kinkily decorated with a propeller on each cup (in honor of her "Flying Nun" role), Sally didn't even bat an eye. She immediately put the bra on over her clothes, began twirling the propellers, and told the cheering college crowd, "Hey, this would make a better television series than the one I did!"

The Harvard gang also felt obliged to draw attention to Sally's recent appearance on the cover of *Playboy* (she had actually posed in a bunny suit). So, two men in pink bunny suits appeared onstage and presented her with a pair of pink rabbit ears. Again Sally, the good sport, took it all in stride. She coquettishly put on the ears, then fetchingly thrust her rear out in the direction of the audience, bumping and grinding like a sophisticated stripper. She finished to a rousing round of applause and whistles.

In one serious moment amidst all the lunacy, Sally harked back to her recent "You really like me" Oscar speech, which had surprised—and hurt—her by resulting in so much flak and ridicule. When the Harvard club presented her with a bean pot (one of their traditional trophies), she said, "At the last award ceremony, I got a lot of heat for the speech I gave. So I'm not going to say anything but thanks."

Some feminists may have decried Sally's decision to pose for a *Playboy* cover, but Sally herself had no regrets. She thought it was all just good, clean fun. She certainly wasn't out to make any sociological statements about the pop pin-up culture, either pro or con, and she was hardly the first female celebrity to pose for Hugh Hefner's magazine. Barbra Streisand had already squeezed into a bunny suit, and a few issues later Joan Collins would reveal a lot more than whiskers and a fuzzy tail.

According to *Playboy* art director Tom Staebler, Sally was a very cooperative subject. "It was unbelievably easy," he said. "She liked the idea." She also felt she was in good company. Inside the magazine, her bunny pictures were part of a frivolous feature on new costume designs at the New York Playboy Club. Those designs included an Indian bunny, a Statue of Liberty bunny, male bunnies (feminists would certainly applaud that!), and a female Michael Jackson look-alike bunny.

Is this the same girl who regularly blushed at Hollywood

parties and actually forced herself to curse like a truckdriver in front of Burt Reynolds, precisely because she feared she was so repressed? No, it can't be—but indeed it is. And that's not all. The Sally Field who feels free enough to pose in a bunny suit is the same Sally Field who now feels confident enough to wheel and deal her way through the hushed inner sanctums of the major movie studios. Her transition from helpless to hard-driving has been nothing short of remarkable, and Sally Field's journey is far from over. Given her success so far, she may wind up president of her own studio—or chairman of a special Presidential commission—before she's through.

Yet despite her enormous success, Sally and her husband, Alan Greisman, continue to live like shopping-mall regulars, not Bel-Air royalty. After all her moves from one part of Los Angeles to another, from Malibu all the way back to Studio City, Sally likes her present home in Tarzana best. She's never been particularly drawn to the posh life of Beverly Hills—she's still a San Fernando Valley girl at heart. Her house looks like a set from one of her old TV sitcoms: There's a basketball hoop over the garage; the doorbell chimes play "The William Tell Overture," and sometimes she waits till April to take down her Christmas lights. With her sons in high school now (and college just around the corner), she's no longer queen of the car-pool set, but she hasn't completely resigned her membership in the suburban homemaking club. Sally still makes dinner every night when she comes home from her production office.

Occasionally, she gives in and allows herself an extravagance or two. She no longer drives the black Trans Am that Burt Reynolds gave her. Instead she has a BMW with a license plate that reads: INSTINKS.

Early in 1987, though, Sally's thoughts turned back to

more practical acquisitions. She began thinking about musical mobiles and baby furniture as she and Alan suddenly found themselves getting ready for a new arrival in the house. The baby—Sally's third—was due in December, shortly after her forty-first birthday and eighteen years after the birth of her first son, Peter. It had been a long time since Sally had mixed formula and changed diapers, but that didn't faze her in the least. She had no qualms about the prospect of raising an infant again, even after such an extended maternity break; nor did she feel the need to take any extra precautions because of her age. In fact, during the first few months of pregnancy, she continued working on *Punchline,* her latest film effort, co-starring Tom Hanks, at a furious pace. She was rushing to finish it up before her condition would start showing on-screen.

As the year drew to a close, Sally had every reason to feel optimistic about her future, both personally and professionally. She had so much to look forward to, and, at the same time, she could look back on the last two decades of her life with a sense of immense satisfaction.

Sally Field made her television debut as Gidget in September 1965. That same season a youngster named Debbie Watson was starring in an equally flimsy sitcom called "Tammy" on ABC, and there were loads of beautiful young actresses on "Petticoat Junction" and "Peyton Place." How many of them ever went on to any kind of enduring fame? Oh yes, a few of the "Peyton Place" girls made a splash for a while—Barbara Parkins and Leigh Taylor-Young each had her moment in the sun—but their careers began to dwindle by the end of the decade. Today, twenty-two years later, of all the "Peyton Place" girls, only Mia Farrow has managed to establish and maintain a lasting film career and her screen accomplishments hardly rival Sally Field's.

Remarkably enough, Sally has even outlasted and outdistanced some of the most dazzling young film actresses of the 1960s—stars like Julie Christie, Samantha Eggar, and Elizabeth Hartman—who were all touted as the new Hepburns and Garbos. Today, they're only half-remembered, while Sally Field remains in the forefront.

What then is the secret of Sally's success? Talent, of course; but in this case tenacity and determination count for much, too. There were so many times when Sally might have given up. Her first TV series, "Gidget," was a flop. Her first screen test, for director Mike Nichols and *The Graduate,* ended in rejection. Her first major film triumph, in *Stay Hungry,* got lost in the shuffle. But Sally's always had a knack for latching onto second chances and making the most of them—in her screen career and in her personal life as well. She's the if-at-first-you-don't-succeed girl who ultimately surpasses all the rest.

Sally once remarked to an interivewer that she didn't feel like Cinderella or Scarlett O'Hara, but like some sort of kookie, magical offspring of them both. She may be right. For it takes the optimism of a Cinderella, and the stubborn willpower of a Scarlett O'Hara, to survive and conquer Hollywood as magnificently as Sally Margaret Field has done.

Index

167